Creative CLIMBERS

Creative CLIMBERS

Inventive planting ideas for every area of the garden

Paul Williams

Special photography by Marianne Majerus

conran
OCTOPUS

For Barbara...mmm...mmm

First published in 1999 by Conran Octopus Limited
37 Shelton Street, London WC2H 9HN
a part of Octopus Publishing Group

COMMISSIONING EDITOR Stuart Cooper
MANAGING EDITOR Catriona Woodburn
EDITORIAL ASSISTANT Paula Hardy
COPY EDITORS Claire Calman, Alison Copland
ART EDITOR Sue Storey
SPECIAL PROJECTS PHOTOGRAPHED BY Marianne Majerus
PICTURE RESEARCH Julia Pashley
PRODUCTION Oliver Jeffreys

A catalogue record for this book is available from the British Library

ISBN 1 85029 945 5

Printed in China

Page 1: Climbers can grow to create a tropical lushness. Ipomoea lobata *and* Cobaea scandens, *raised as annuals from
seed, quickly envelop trellis or fences with a colourful, luxuriant covering.*

Pages 2–3: Rosa *'Iceberg' enjoys full sun and open, airy conditions. Here its double flowers contrast
with the white starburst flowers of* Crambe cordifolia, *seen catching the sun in the distance.*

*Page 5: Climbers can be used to conceal the unsightly or embellish the functional. Nasturtiums (*Tropaeolum majus*)
complement the rustic scene and give colour and style to an otherwise plain dog kennel.*

Contents

Introduction

Climbing plants provide a huge diversity of texture, flower, shape, colour and scent. They range in size from vast tree-climbing vines and vigorous, all-smothering climbing roses to delicate tender annuals. Climbers can be used to clothe structures, softening their harsh outlines, or to form a colourful living screen between contrasting areas of the garden.

A wide range of supports for climbing plants is now available, and these provide the gardener with the opportunity for creating lively boundaries and divisions such as walls and fences, as well as free-standing structures such as pergolas and arbours. Climbers can also enhance living supports, growing and flowering through the branches of mature trees, or entwining in a young hedge. Combinations of different climbing plants, with their varying flowering times, can be cleverly used to create an extended season of interest for an otherwise dull corner of the garden. Climbers provide vertical growth in the garden, and so open up a world of design possibilities.

LEFT: *The natural grace of wisteria can be appreciated best when the plant is allowed to grow freely through trees. Its flowering coincides with that of* **Cornus kousa,** *creating a harmonious blend of lilac and white.*

H EIGHT IS AN IMPORTANT, and often neglected, element in garden design. In a small garden, in particular, the use of vertical spaces greatly increases the number and variety of plants that can be grown. The tall growth of climbers can be used to lead the eye around the garden, drawing attention to certain features by framing them with foliage. Alternatively, ornamental supports for climbers to grow on, such as pyramids and obelisks, can be used to create symmetry, perspective, or as a striking focal point. Climbers can also be used to mask unsightly objects and, of course, to provide respite from the sun in the form of, say, a pergola draped in roses or clematis, or a vine-covered terrace.

Designing with Climbers

ABOVE: A *romantic pairing of roses and honeysuckle (Lonicera) viewed through diamond trellis.*
LEFT: *The large leaves of Hedera colchica 'Dentata Variegata' on this arch create a striking surround to the view of red-hot pokers (Kniphofia).*

COLOUR

Colour themes or simple colour combinations are an important part of a garden's make-up and show a consideration of design that will set a garden apart from the rest. Climbers can contribute both by enhancing colour schemes and by lengthening the season of colour. The use of colour in the garden extends not just to the plants but also to the buildings and structures that form the background to the garden planting.

Choice of colours is highly subjective. Some people prefer white with pastel pinks and blues, while others are excited by bright oranges and reds. Use of gentler colours creates a romantic effect, whereas use of fiery colours in, say, a sun-filled border, creates a more stimulating response. These are two extremes of colour use, but elements of each can be combined with the other to tone down or enliven a scheme.

There is a debate about whether the warm reds at the yellow end of the red spectrum (such as those found in nasturtiums) should be grown with cooler reds with more blue in them – colours heading towards violet and magenta (such as those of *Clematis* 'Ernest Markham' and *C.* 'Madame Julia Correvon'). In general I would recommend that such mixtures be avoided; however, if care is taken to consider the proportions of one colour to another, their relative tones, and the shape and texture of the flowers (which can affect the impact of the colour), some startling and vibrant combinations can be achieved. For example, the bright orange, daisy-like flowers of the tender *Senecio confusus* grown during the summer through the purple leaves of *Cotinus coggygria* 'Royal Purple' makes a vivid show.

This breaks the practice of not planting yellow-reds with blue-reds, but the purple-tinged leaves and stems of the senecio blend in with the cotinus, and the lively flowers succeed because of their brilliance.

It is important to consider the colour of climbers when using them as background in borders, when growing them together, or when allowing them to scramble through mixed planting of shrubs and perennials. Plants on a wall or fence at the back of a border have a great effect on the plants in front; for instance, a bed of *Rosa* 'Iceberg' will make twice the impression when backed by the leaves of *Vitis vinifera* 'Purpurea', particularly when the two entangle and the white flowers nestle on a bed of deep burgundy leaves. Similarly, a backdrop of the variegated ivy *Hedera colchica* 'Sulphur Heart' will show up the darker leaves of *Physocarpus* 'Diabolo'.

Foliage shrubs like cornus can be 'given' flowers by growing climbers through them. Try *Cornus alba* 'Aurea' with the flame flower (*Tropaeolum speciosum*) for a really startling combination of lime-green leaves and vivid red flowers. For a more subtle yet equally effective look, try the rich burgundy of *Clematis* 'Royal Velours' grown through the velvety, silver leaves of *Buddleja fallowiana*.

Spring-flowering shrubs can be given a second season by planting a late-flowering climber to come up through them. The dense greenery of choisya, with its highly fragrant white flowers borne in early summer, can be used to support the fresh yellow flowers of canary creeper (*Tropaeolum peregrinum*), which will appear right up until the onset of frosts.

In autumn, there are several climbers that shake off their subdued greens to put on the most fiery and spectacular display of colours. The scarlet and crimson of Virginia creeper (*Parthenocissus quinquefolia*) glowing in low sunshine is a glorious sight. Other climbers with good autumn colour include *Vitis coignetiae*, which has plate-sized leaves that turn a bronzy red, and *V. amurensis*, whose large palmate leaves make bold splashes of red. A softer look is created by the warm, butter-yellow autumn leaves of *Celastrus orbiculatus*. This is a plant happy to twine its way into a tree where its impact is far greater than when grown against a wall. In addition, the female plant produces handsome, orange-red berries in autumn.

ABOVE: *The half-hardy Abutilon megapotamicum trails its last branches over a rose.*
LEFT: *Vines give brilliant autumn colours. These pillars offer a grand scale and warm background colour to the reddened leaves of Vitis coignetiae.*

GROWING CLIMBERS TOGETHER

Many climbing plants have just one flowering season and can be dull at other times of the year. By growing different climbers together, a more prolonged display can be achieved.

Combining climbers and matching them to a colour-themed border can create stunning, extended displays. A border of blue and pink in early to midsummer which gradually develops reds and yellows as crocosmias and rudbeckias appear, can be enriched by growing the early-summer, pink, climbing *Rosa* 'Madame Grégoire Staechelin'

Another exciting idea is to match climbers that flower at the same time. Try growing the purple *Clematis* 'The President' through the early, rich yellow *Rosa* 'Maigold' for a bright and cheerful mix. Deadheading the rose will produce another flush of flowers later to coincide with the large, violet-blue flowers of *Clematis* 'Ascotiensis' and a second flush from *C*. 'The President'.

Sweet peas (*Lathyrus odoratus*) are ideal for growing up through *Clematis montana*. Trim the clematis straight after flowering in late spring, then plant the sweet peas for more colour.

LEFT: *The autumn colours of* **Vitis coignetiae** *show up brightly against* **Hedera helix.**
RIGHT: *Different flower shapes can work well together. Here the delicate honeysuckle flowers offset the larger blooms of the clematis.*

behind it. The rose hips turn orange as the season pro-gresses, and can be complemented by the late, orange flowers of the leafy *Eccremocarpus scaber*, which will also cover the rose's bare lower stems.

Similar plants of different shades grown together make subtle combinations; for example, the large-flowered, purple *Clematis* 'Jackmanii', grown with a darker or lighter shade of clematis such as *C*. 'Perle d'Azur' or *C*. 'Gipsy Queen', produces a blend of colours that gives the impression of flowers fading as they mature. In the spring, this effect can be produced with *C. alpina* 'Frances Rivis', *C. alpina* 'Pamela Jackman' and *C. alpina* 'Columbine'.

SHAPES AND PATTERNS

Climbers are usually thought of as somewhat wild and wayward plants, but some of them can be 'tamed' to produce formal geometric shapes.

A neat and easy way to create patterns on walls or against fences is to train ivy on trellis shapes. These can be traditional squares or diamonds, or perhaps bold zigzags. Alternatively, create simple upright lines with spaced wooden battens. Shapes can, for example, be created to echo arches or windows in the architecture of the house, or other garden structures. To make a pattern with curved lines against a wall, use wire and screw eyes instead of battens. In frost-free climates, ivy can be replaced with creeping fig (*Ficus pumila*).

When grown as a standard, ivy forms interesting shapes. Train three or more leading shoots upright, using a cane for early support, by twisting or plaiting them. Let them grow to 1m (3ft) high, then pinch out the tips to produce a bushy head. Remove all sideshoots from the stems below the head. As the stems thicken, they form a gnarled trunk for this ivy 'tree'. Wisterias and honeysuckles can also be developed in this way.

Growing climbers as espaliers is one means of overcoming the problem of limited space. An unlikely candidate for this growing method is *Clematis montana*. Normally seen as a rampant climber smothered in flowers during early summer, it can be trained to grow in a more restrained way along wires, to produce neat 'arms' packed solid with scented flowers. Fix horizontal wires 45cm

RIGHT: *Ivies can be trained to frame doors and windows. They also provide invaluable support for other climbers.*

(18in) or so apart on a wall or fence, and plant the clematis in the middle or at either end of the wires. If it already has more than one shoot, train each one along a different wire; otherwise, train the single stem horizontally along the bottom wire. As new shoots arise, leave one near the base to grow up. Pinch back any new shoots along the horizontal stem, but leave the end one to extend the growth. When the vertical shoot has grown long enough, tie it to the next wire. Repeat this process to cover all the wires. The shoots can be extended a considerable distance along walls or around windows. Try to keep the wires within reach, as regular pinching out will be required to keep the growth tight and compact. The effect is well worth the effort.

ABOVE: *Ivy clipped tightly to an open trellis softens the lines and adds texture. Here it also provides an interesting background to a lively and colourful spring planting.*

SCENTED CLIMBERS

Plant and train climbers where their scent will be most appreciated. The long fragrant trails of *Wisteria sinensis* hanging from a pergola are more readily smelt than when hung high on a wall. The same applies to roses – those growing on arbours and arches bring the scent directly to the nose. Climbers around windows and doorways allow the scent to drift into the house. In frost-free climates, *Mandevilla laxa* will provide a rich fragrance.

There is a long list of scented climbing and rambling roses, from the prolific and extremely vigorous – 13m (42ft) or more – *Rosa* 'Bobbie James', with its small, creamy-white flowers, to the altogether more petite – 3m (10ft) – *R.* 'Phyllis Bide', which has small, yellow flowers and, most unusually for a rambler, is repeat-flowering. There is a wide range of colours to choose from in the scented roses, from the double, crimson-purple flowers of *R.* 'Russelliana' to the large, clear yellow flowers of *R.* 'Lawrence Johnston', a robust plant with shiny, deep green foliage.

Honeysuckles are another group of plants with good scents, but those with the showiest of flowers often have no scent at all. The flowers of the sweetly scented *Lonicera* × *americana* are a rich rose and cream in colour, ideal when grown with the buff and pink flowers of *Rosa* 'Gloire de Dijon'. Two cultivars of the wild woodbine (*L. periclymenum* 'Belgica' and 'Serotina'), will between them provide flowers right through the season, while the creamy-yellow *L. periclymenum* 'Graham Thomas' flowers through to late autumn. All of these are at their most fragrant in the evening.

One of the most powerful scents in the garden comes from the jasmines. *Jasminum officinale* is a vigorous climber that can produce an abundance of flowers. Sometimes, however, scents can be most alluring when lightly chanced upon. Climbing plants with insignificant flowers but heavy scents can be used among other plants to provide subtler hints of fragrance. *Akebia quinata* is such a plant,

RIGHT: **Plant Rosa 'Paul's Himalayan Musk' near seating or over an arbour where its lightly scented flowers can be enjoyed at close quarters.**

with grey-purple flowers hidden among its leaves. *Holboellia coriacea*, with inconspicuous, green-white flowers, is another.

Scented annual climbers are in rather short supply. Sweet peas are better appreciated as cut flowers, where their attractive blooms can be concentrated in a single vase.

CLIMBING VEGETABLES AND FRUIT

The kitchen garden is often regarded as the functional area of the garden, resulting in regimented rows of plants interspersed with climbers grown on traditional supports, such as wigwams for runner beans and espalier apples and pears. Good productivity, however, can be combined with creativity by using structures more usually seen in the formal ornamental garden. Tripods, pyramids, arches, pergolas and tunnels can all be used to great effect, giving the kitchen garden unusual visual interest.

ABOVE: *The autumn leaves of* **Vitis vinifera** *'Purpurea' offset the bunches of fruit.*
RIGHT: *Marrows can be trained over an arch to produce a stunning display.*

A pergola is an ideal support for vigorous blackberry plants. The blackberry has the same growth pattern as a rambler rose. Long shoots arise in one season, then flower and fruit the next. While the current season's flowers are on show, the stems that will flower in the following year are growing rapidly. So each year, once the fruit is gathered, cut out the old stems completely and tie in the new shoots. Against a wall or shed they can be tied into arching or wavy patterns, which look effective in the winter when their forms are leafless. Thornless blackberries are easier to manage, and have the bonus of possessing finely cut leaves. For a mixed, fruity walkway alternate plantings of grape vines and blackberries are a good combination.

Regularly placed tripods of cane or hazel along a pathway, each planted with a different climbing bean, adds a touch of grandeur to the vegetable plot. Contrast the red-flowered runner bean 'Royal Standard' with the white-flowered 'Desirée'; or try 'Painted Lady', which has red and white blossoms. For a colourful combination, use the climbing French bean 'Marvel of Venice', which has broad yellow pods, with the Italian 'Viola Cornetti', which bears purple-podded beans.

Pumpkins, especially the small-fruited, trailing ones such as 'Jack Be Little' and the slightly larger 'Blue Kuri' with its striking blue-grey skin, are an exciting addition when hung with their exotic-looking fruit in the autumn. Encourage them up a tripod or over an arch for best effect, and tie in where necessary.

Though not strictly climbers, cherry tomatoes can be trained up a cane and will crop over a long period. Two tall types with excellent flavour are 'Gardener's Delight' and 'Harbinger' (a variety

which has the advantage that any green tomatoes will ripen well off the plant). They will need lots of water and food, and a good deal of sunshine.

By adopting an allotment style in the vegetable garden, all sorts of liberties can be taken. Use old ladders, bed frames and bicycle wheels to mimic the constructions in more formal parts of the garden. Some judicious touches of paint will prevent it from looking like a scrapyard.

CLIMBERS AS GROUND COVER

The vigour of climbers can be exploited by diverting their energies from the vertical to the horizontal to make a dense, weed-smothering carpet of ground cover.

For dark and shady places where little else will grow, ivies are a good choice. They need not be dull if variegated or pale-leaved types are used, and are ideal for lightening shaded areas. *Hedera colchica* 'Sulphur Heart' has large, dark green leaves, each with a lime-yellow centre. It makes a stunning sight with snowdrops (Galanthus) and purple hellebores pushing through it in the spring. *H. colchica* 'Dentata Variegata' is another boldly variegated, large-leaved ivy with a creamy-yellow colouring. A much smaller one is *H. helix* 'Glacier', which has grey and white variegation. It combines well with snowdrops, and is good as an underplanting to bronze- or purple-leaved plants such as *Heuchera micrantha diversifolia* 'Palace Purple'. Most pale-leaved ivies turn green in the shade.

Ivy has the advantage that, as it spreads, it puts down roots that bind and stabilize banks and make for denser growth. It is good for disguising ugly manhole covers, and revives well if it should have to be cut back in order to gain access.

More colourful ground cover, for spring through to autumn, can be provided by clematis, which, if given no support, will spread across the ground. Unsupported clematis tend to cling on to their own stems and make a tangled mass. Choosing plants from the *viticella* and *texensis* groups makes for easier maintenance. These can be cut hard back in late winter or early spring, and the tangled stems removed wholesale. Plants from the small-leaved *viticella* group make a remarkable late-summer carpet. For a large area, the vigorous *Clematis* 'Alba Luxurians' takes some beating, with its exceptionally long flowering period. Try mixing its frothy white flowers with the rich deep purple of *C.* 'Etoile Violette'.

For spring, cultivars of *Clematis alpina* provide a range of colour from pink to lavender-blue and white. On their own, they do not provide such a

dense, weedproof cover as ivy; however, the flowers can be shown off to great effect if grown over a green ivy carpet. *C. alpina* cultivars also flower well in shade.

Some climbing clematis have been hybridized with their herbaceous relatives, giving rise to plants with large flowers and a scrambling habit – good for ground cover. One of the most outstanding is *Clematis* × *durandii*. It has large, indigo-violet flowers, produced from midsummer onwards, that combine well with the yellow blooms of *Crocosmia* 'Golden Fleece' or *Hemerocallis* 'Golden Chimes'.

Two unlikely, but successful, ground-cover plants are Virginia creeper and Boston ivy (*Parthenocissus tricuspidata*) ; both are extremely vigorous but provide dense, glossy foliage that eventually colours to brilliant red and crimson in autumn. Their spread can be controlled by cutting off the leading shoots with shears, or by running a rotary lawn mower on a high setting, or a nylon-line trimmer, over them.

GROWING CLIMBERS IN POTS

For those with only a paved area, roof or balcony in which to create their garden, the easiest – and often the only – solution is to grow plants in pots and planters. Use a quality soil-based compost with a good supply of fertilizers. The length of time before a plant needs repotting depends on the vigour of the plant and the size of the container.

LEFT: *Strands of honeysuckle weave through the stems of* Sisyrinchium striatum.
RIGHT: *Using a tangle of stems as support, an ivy-leaved pelargonium scrambles up a mass of pink asarina to smother this arch.*

Poor growth and yellowing leaves are indications that the compost is running out of nutrients. Liquid feeding will provide an immediate, short-term remedy, but repotting should follow as soon as possible. Provided that there is regular feeding, repotting, and removal and replacement of some of the compost around the roots, surprisingly large plants can be grown in containers. Wisteria, for example, if well fed, can be grown as a standard or trained along a balcony rail.

Larger pots will produce bigger and healthier plants, and judicious pruning will keep the more vigorous subjects in check. Smaller plants are easier to care for, and, if free-standing with their own supports, can be moved around, allowing you to maintain an interesting and changing display. Rows of identical pots with tall supports make a strong design feature. Mixing climbers in pots with other shrubs and perennials allows you to recreate the richness and variety of a garden border.

There are various ways to support plants in pots. If the pot is at the foot of a wall, all the usual means of support, such as wires and trellis, can be used. If the pot is free-standing, the simplest method is to push three or four garden canes into the pot and tie them, wigwam-style, at the top. With a traditionally shaped pot, push the canes in deep, down the sides, so that they angle outwards from the pot. When they are gently bent inwards at the top and tied together, an elegant, curved shape is formed.

Bamboo canes can be very smooth, making it difficult for some plants, such as nasturtiums and sweet peas, to get an initial hold. Instead you could try hazel poles or other rough sticks cut from the garden. Binding the canes around with coloured

string at intervals makes them ornamental and also helps the plant to grip. Long willow stems make good supports, and their suppleness enables them to be bent into various shapes, creating attractive, curvaceous designs in the garden.

Wire is a useful and flexible material. A heavy-gauge wire formed into a spiral and held up in the centre by a cane is ideal for making *faux* topiary from ivy. And tall wire loops over a pot make elegant supports for annuals.

More elaborate supports, such as pyramids or obelisks made from wooden battens, can be placed on Versaille planters to give them extra height while still maintaining their formal character.

There are certain vigorous plants that are better grown in pots. These include some invasive spreaders such as the pink, double-flowered *Calystegia hederacea* 'Flore Pleno' and the dainty-leaved *Convolvulus althaeoides*. Tender and half-hardy plants that need extra care during winter are also easier to manage when grown in pots that can be brought into the protective environment of a greenhouse, conservatory or frost-free garage.

A regular crop of fresh vegetables can be produced from the tiniest balcony. Make the most of the vertical space by growing runner beans, climbing French beans, peas, cherry tomatoes and (in very sheltered conditions) cucumbers.

Grapes can also be grown successfully in pots. Do not expect a vast crop, but train them on a simple frame and keep the vines small by regular pruning and pinching out.

LEFT: *Tender plants like* **Ipomoea lobata** *should be kept in a warm environment until well established. Then they can be moved outdoors.*

Climbers under Glass

Offering plants the sheltered environment of a greenhouse or conservatory opens up the possibility of growing a range of exotic plants, many of them vigorous and most of them responsive to pruning. Tender climbers can be grown with an underplanting of tender shrubs for a tropical atmosphere.

Running a heated conservatory need not mean expensive heating bills. If the plants are chosen carefully, you can still have an exotic-looking scheme with a winter temperature only just above freezing. Plants like the parrot's bill (*Clianthus puntceus*), with clusters of bright red, claw-like flowers, and *Hardenbergia comptoniana,* with its showy racemes of purple pea flowers, are tolerant of cool winter temperatures. Relatives of the convolvulus, morning glories (*Ipomoea* species), although happy outside in frost-free climates, appreciate the extra warmth of a conservatory in those areas where summer takes a little time to warm up, and will produce a better show of flowers. The same applies to other climbers that are on the borderline of hardiness, such as *Solanum jasminoides* 'Album'.

For supporting climbing plants in conservatories, the house wall is the easiest place to fix wires or mesh. In larger conservatories, free-standing plants can be grown up wires running from the pot to the roof support. Sections of trellis can be secured in the pot and wired to the roof for extra support. A cane tripod pushed into the pot makes a simple and effective support for less vigorous climbers. The stronger, more vigorous climbers can be used as support for more delicate plants such as *Tweedia caerulea* (*Oxypetalum caeruleum*).

ABOVE: *A lushness of tropical flora, such as this showy* **Clianthus puniceus** *with its parrot's-bill flowers, is readily created in a conservatory.*

Growing plants in raised beds open to the soil below allows plenty of space for the roots to spread and they do not need such regular watering as those confined in pots.

TYPES OF CLIMBER

Understanding how each climbing plant attaches itself will help you establish it successfully on a wall, fence or other support. It is important to distinguish between true climbers and wall shrubs. Once established, and given the right structure to climb on, true climbers will hold on unaided. Plants such as ceanothus, garryas and pyracanthas are wall shrubs, and need training and tying in because they have no natural method of attaching themselves to a support.

tropaeolums use a similar principle, but in these cases it is the leaf stem that curls around the support. Certain plants like mutisias and littonias use tendrils at the ends of their leaves.

With twining plants, the leading shoot twists itself around any vertical support as the plant grows. Examples include runner beans, honeysuckles, wisteria and bindweed (*Convolvulus* species).

Smaller climbers, with fine tendrils, need fairly narrow supports such as mesh or twigs, while the more vigorous types, such as vines, can get their

LEFT: *Tendrils will wind around branches as seen in the habit of the* Cucurbita *family.*
RIGHT: *The twining shoots of* Lablab purpureus *grow through and around supports.*

TENDRILS AND TWINERS

Many plants climb by means of tendrils, which search out something to grip on to, and then gradually wind themselves around it. Good examples include the grape vine and its relatives (*Vitis* species) and sweet peas. Clematis and

tendrils around larger branches and trellis. If planting tendril or twining climbers against a wall or fence, however, they will require additional means of support. Tie them initially to a framework of wide-gauge mesh or vertical wires.

When mature, vigorous plants like wisteria or honeysuckle can crush trellis and push drainpipes away from a wall, so resist the temptation to tuck their shoots behind exterior pipework. Check for shoots that are pushing up under roof tiles and cut back to at least 1m (3ft) below the eaves.

SCRAMBLERS AND RAMBLERS

Brambles seem to scramble through bushes without any obvious adaptation for climbing. A closer look, however, reveals the presence of thorns. These point downwards, gripping the host, and they stop the plant from slipping. Blackberries produce vigorous, thorny shoots that flower and fruit the following year, and they use the hummocks of the previous year's growth as support. Rambling and climbing species roses grow by the same method. Where gardeners cut away the previous

SELF-CLINGERS

The most common self-clinger is ivy, which holds on by means of a mass of aerial roots along the length of its stems. These roots exude a glutinous substance and 'glue' themselves to the surface. A more intriguing method is employed by Virginia creepers (*Parthenocissus* species). Each shoot splits into smaller shoots, every one with a small disc at the end which sticks to the wall. The tendrils then contract, pulling the stem close to the surface.

LEFT: *Blackberries scramble by means of thorns which lodge in other plants for support.*
RIGHT: **Parthenocissus tricuspidata grips onto its support by sticking its tendril tips onto the wall.**

year's growth they have to provide alternative support in the form of an arbour or pergola.

Other plants, such as winter-flowering jasmine (*Jasminum nudiflorum*), simply use their vigorous, wiry shoots to scramble their way upwards, leaning on any available support.

On stone or brick walls that are in good condition, self-clingers pose no problem, but where cracks exist the searching shoots of ivy will find their way in and may cause damage. Plants that are self-clinging can be among the most difficult to get started; they need to be held firm and still against the surface so that the aerial roots or tendrils have a chance to fix themselves. Once firmly established, however, they are the easiest to manage. They need a sound surface that is neither flaky nor dusty.

CULTIVATION AND CARE

The ease with which most climbers can be grown makes them reliable and effective plants for the garden. As with all plants, a little extra care taken at planting time will get them off to a flying start.

SITING

Some climbers have special requirements, an obvious example being the clematis with its need for a cool root run. Applying a thick organic mulch, or planting the clematis with its roots in the shade of shrubs, helps to overcome this problem.

A less obvious example is the brilliantly coloured flame flower. Its air of fragility suggests that it needs a warm, sunny wall, yet what it really enjoys is a cool position with some moisture. The Chilean glory vine (*Eccremocarpus scaber*), with a similar exotic look and climbing habit, needs warmth and enjoys full sunshine.

The protection afforded by a house wall can create a microclimate that is a few degrees warmer than the surrounding garden, making it possible to grow plants which would perish elsewhere, such as campsis, mutisias and *Tropaeolum tuberosum*.

A surprising number of climbers tolerate shady conditions; examples include *Hydrangea anomala petiolaris*, schisandras, schizophragmas and ivies. The vigorous *Clematis montana* will produce a mass of flowers even on a wall that never gets sun. *Parthenocissus henryana* becomes an altogether more classy plant in the shade, where its silver-grey leaf-vein markings are more pronounced. On the

RIGHT: *This open-air shower, draped in greenery, provides enough privacy for comfort without spoiling the liberating feeling of the outdoors.*

other hand, the startling pink, white and green leaves of *Actinidia kolomikta* are more vivid, and wisteria flowers are more prolific, when these plants are grown in a sunny position.

PLANTING

Any plant bought in a pot can be planted at any time of the year, provided the ground is neither waterlogged nor frozen, although autumn, when the soil is warm and moist, is usually best.

Freshly planted young climbers are at risk from drying out and wind damage, and this is where good preparation of the planting site will be most beneficial. Dig a hole at least twice as deep and wide as the pot containing the plant. Loosen the soil in the bottom of the hole to help drainage and aid root penetration. Work some organic material (such as rotted grass cuttings, manure or compost) into this soil. If the sides of the hole have been smoothed by the spade, break them up with a fork to allow roots to spread sideways easily.

Soak the plant in its pot by placing in a bucket of water for about an hour before planting. Then position the plant so that its 'neck' is at the same level in the soil as it was in the pot. Mix organic material with the soil from the hole. Use this to refill, adding a bit at a time and gently firming it as you go. The organic material provides nutrients, keeps the soil open, and helps with moisture retention. Always water the plant in thoroughly.

In frost-prone regions, plants that are of borderline hardiness, such as *Solanum crispum* and *Eccremocarpus scaber*, are better planted in spring, which gives them a whole growing season to establish themselves. Plant them 5–8cm (2–3in) deeper than usual, in a slight hollow. As the season progresses, gradually cover the stem with a few centimetres of soil. This will enable regrowth from the base if they are knocked back by frosts.

Good preparation is particularly important when planting against walls. It is often recommended that you position climbers 50–60cm (20–24in) away from the foot of the wall to keep the plant out of the dry zone. This is certainly good practice, but it can make it difficult to establish the plant against the wall, particularly plants that are self-clinging. It may be necessary to grow plants up a cane until the stems are long enough to be bent over and attached to the wall. Any movement from strong winds will prevent self-clinging plants from attaching themselves to the wall. For this reason, it is essential to use sturdy canes (and lead-headed nails when attaching to walls).

ABOVE: *Plant climbers at a distance from a post to prevent the post being loosened when the hole is dug. New shoots can be trained across on a cane.*

Using hedges, trees and shrubs as supports for climbers poses particular problems when planting, and this is dealt with in the chapter 'Living Supports' (see page 74).

Once a climber has established itself you may need to tie in the new shoots to the plant's support. If you use nylon or wire to tie in, be sure to check regularly, as the stems thicken, that the ties are not too tight. String is preferable. When tying in plants, first tie the cord to the support, then fasten it around the plant stem.

WATERING AND FEEDING

Check newly planted climbers regularly for drying out, and water them as needed. A thick organic mulch applied annually will help reduce water loss and has the advantage of feeding the plant as well as keeping the soil damp. There are mulch mats available which have this moisture-retaining ability. Fork in an occasional feed of a general-purpose fertilizer when the soil is moist. Any plant that is undernourished will send all available

nitrogen (the element needed for growth) to the top of the plant at the expense of the lower leaves, which may fall off if starved for too long.

'BARE LEGS'

When growth is concentrated at the top, leaves cannot survive further down, leaving the lower part looking bare and unattractive. To prevent this happening, ensure that the entire plant receives plenty of light and is not shaded by its own straggly upper growth; this can be achieved by careful pruning and trimming.

If 'bare legs' cannot be avoided, there are three ways of dealing with the problem: encouraging new growth from the base of the plant by means of hard pruning; making a feature of the bare stems; and clothing the stems with other plants.

Climbing roses will respond well to some of the older shoots being cut back almost to the base during winter. Vigorous new shoots will then appear in spring. Jasmine and honeysuckle will respond to drastic pruning in late spring; cut them right back, near to ground level, encouraging strong new shoots to appear. *Clematis montana*, however, will not respond to such treatment; an overgrown specimen is best replaced with a young plant, which should be pruned regularly, after flowering, to keep it compact.

The trunks of some robust climbers have qualities worth showing off. For example, the trunks of *Lonicera hildebrandiana* bear papery exfoliations and *Aristolochia macrophylla* makes a

LEFT: *When tying in new shoots, tie the string first to the support and then around the stem in order to prevent stems rubbing or being crushed.*

tangled jumble of stems with a surface ruptured by raised lenticels. On *Hydrangea anomala petiolaris* the remains of the adventitious roots give the young branches a rough, hairy appearance, while the older trunks develop deep, rough ridges of stacked, papery bark.

'Bare legs' may be covered with other plants. If you plant a small-leaved ivy, such as *Hedera helix* 'Duckfoot' or *H. helix* 'Merion Beauty', at the base of the climber, you can train the leading shoots of the ivy up the bare stems of the climber, following its twists and turns. The shoots will need tying in at first. Pinch them off at the required height, and keep them clipped tight to the stem to reduce their vigour and keep the effect of a green wrapping. This method is suitable for the thick stems of *Clematis montana*. For climbing roses and wisteria, it will be necessary to remove any twiggy growth, leaving a clean stem for the ivy to grow up.

PRUNING

As climbers are so diverse a group of plants, it is impossible to give any general pruning advice. Refer to individual entries in the Plant Directory (page 83) for any special pruning requirements.

CARING FOR TENDER CLIMBERS

In frost-prone areas, *Solanum jasminoides* and its white form 'Album' can be overwintered indoors as cuttings or small plants, then planted out when all danger of frost has passed. You can do the same with the blue-flowered Cape leadwort (*Plumbago auriculata*); its scrambling shoots will push through shrubs to hold aloft clusters of sky-blue flowers right up to the first frosts.

ABOVE: *The bare stem of a vine provides a fine support for nasturtiums .*

Some tender climbers are worth growing as specimens in their own right. You can either take them out of the greenhouse or conservatory in summer and place them, in their pots, against a wall or trellis, or, for easier maintenance and greater vigour, take them out of their pots and plant them directly in the ground lifting them again at the end of the season. These plants include the very elegant, orange-yellow flowers of *Tropaeolum tuberosum lineamaculatum* 'Ken Aslet', which has edible tubers; the Canary Island bellflower (*Canarina canariensis*); and the bright orange-flowered marmalade bush (*Streptosolen jamesonii*).

WALLS, FENCES and other dividing structures play a dual role in the garden, combining functionality with an opportunity for decoration. In pracitcal terms they form demarcation lines and barriers between the garden and the world beyond, as well as separating different areas within the garden to create pockets of interest. However, they also form valuable supports for a wide range of climbers, allowing for imaginative planting within the garden, and the potential to lead the eye cleverly from one feature to another. Making use of the surface areas of house – and other – walls, fences and similar boundaries can greatly increase the density of plant growth in a small garden.

Boundaries and Divisions

ABOVE: *Boundary walls can be softened with plants such as* **Lonicera periclymenum 'Graham Thomas'**.
LEFT: *Seen through open trellis, catmint (Nepeta), forms a contrasting background for the climbing* **Rosa 'Souvenir du Docteur Jamain'**.

WALLS

Walls allow no light to penetrate through, and consequently create dense shade; they retain heat, thus offering protection to plants; and although they can cause turbulence in windy areas, they protect plants from rain. They offer varied and distinct growing conditions in the garden, and this should be considered when choosing plants to grow up or beside them.

The type of wall has considerable influence on the style of the garden and the planting. White stucco is an ideal background for creating formal shapes; while the colour and texture of red brick complements the colours of most plants, particularly warm reds and yellows. The blue-black engineering brick makes a very dark background. Left bare, it is an ideal setting for steely blue, purple and white, but it can be greened up with evergreens, such as ivy, to become the background for other climbing plants.

Honey-coloured Cotswold stone, like brick, sandstone and ironstone, is an easy surface to work with. Its mellow tones provide a sympathetic background for a wide range of colours.

The mottled greys and hints of brown in flint walling, along with its irregular shape, make a busy surface. This can be a feature in itself; otherwise it needs bold foliage that is not going to be lost in the confusion of colour and texture.

There are numerous styles of dry-stone walling. These are invariably built with stone from the local landscape, and their natural look is ideal for informal planting. Remember that there is no mortar holding these walls together and that therefore they may become unstable if infiltrated

LEFT: *Twigs pushed into the cracks in dry stone walls will help climbers to attach themselves.*
RIGHT: *The abundant flowers and graceful habit of rambling roses help to soften solid walls.*

by the questing stems of climbers such as ivy. Less damaging climbers, such as clematis and some lathyrus, are more suitable.

ATTACHING CLIMBERS TO WALLS

Climbers that are not self-clinging must be attached to the wall in some way. Trellis is one of the best supports for climbers; for advice on how to attach trellis to a wall, see page 34.

Another simple method is to bang in a nail where needed, and tie the plant to it with string. Lead-headed nails have a lead tag attached to the head which can be bent over a stem to hold it against the wall. The lead becomes brittle with age, but is very good for holding young shoots to get them established.

Rather than knock nails in randomly, it is tidier and more convenient to fix permanent wires, either horizontally or vertically, about 23–30cm (9–12in) apart. You can then tie in the plants to the wires as required. Where possible, use plastic-coated or galvanized wire to prevent rusting. On very long runs, use nylon monofilament, as used by fruit-growers, as it does not stretch and sag. Attach the wire or nylon filament by screw-eyes, drilled and plugged into the wall, or by vine-eyes hammered into the joints between bricks every 90cm (3ft). Get the wire as tight as you can by gripping it with pliers and pulling it through the eye. While still pulling, bend it back over the eye, then wrap it securely around itself.

An alternative to wire is to use bamboo canes, or narrow rustic poles, wired to the eyes. These can be fixed vertically or horizontally. They present a structural form during winter when stems are bare, or when annual climbers have died down.

ABOVE: *This impressive display of* **Lathyrus latifolius** *is supported by strong wire mesh* **attached to the gable end.**

Nylon mesh is a very good support for climbers and avoids the damage to dry stone walls that can be caused by hammering in numerous pegs. Plastics often look out of place in the garden, so choose a dark-coloured mesh that will be unobtrusive; or match it to the colour of the wall. Attach it to the wall by fixing it first to a wooden frame, or by a screw and a large washer in the corner of each mesh square.

Rendering is applied to walls to provide a waterproof skin, so it is not advisable either to drill or to knock nails into it.

Establishing plants against a wall can pose certain problems and these are dealt with in 'Cultivation and Care' on page 24.

Climbing plants growing on a wall facing the prevailing wind will experience particularly high wind speeds because the air gets pushed along the face of the wall. Fixing trellis 45–60cm (18–24in) high along the top of a wall will help to disperse some of the wind force blowing over it.

BOUNDARY FENCES

Fences are the ideal garden boundary from the point of view of a plant's welfare. Unlike hedges, they take no goodness from the ground, and they do not have the same drying effect as a wall.

A picket fence provides a good barrier, but can easily be made more of by shaping the top of the rails, adjusting the space between the rails, or painting it in a colour that complements the surrounding buildings or the accompanying planting.

Post-and-rail fences have a functional construction and it is difficult to make them look attractive. Sturdily built, designed to keep out large livestock, they will stand being planted with vigorous plants

that will mask their uninspiring appearance. A plant that I would hesitate to recommend for any other situation, because it is so rampant, but which is ideally suited here, is the enormous *Rosa filipes* 'Kiftsgate', with its large, dramatic clusters of single, fragrant, creamy-white flowers. Training it horizontally instead of vertically makes it more accessible for pruning, and its scent can be more readily appreciated.

Woven hazel hurdles give a rustic effect. For durability, choose those made from whole stems, as split stems expose the interior of the wood to weathering and shorten its life considerably.

Wooden fences will, from time to time, need treating with a preservative. Often the easiest option is to cut the plants hard back (most climbers will tolerate this treatment) and cover them with a plastic sheet while you apply the preservative. If the plants are on wires along the fence, removing the wires will make it easier. Be certain to choose a proprietary brand of preservative that is not harmful to plants.

Woodwork treated with woodstain and preservative provides a more practical solution to colouring wood than paint. These products soak into the wood and do not peel or crack. Do not plant climbers at the foot of wooden posts, as these may have to be replaced from time to time.

By growing evergreens, such as *Lonicera henryi* or *Trachelospermum asiaticum*, up free-standing trellis, a hedge-like effect can be achieved.

Trellis used as a boundary fence, or as an internal screen (see page 35), should be attached to posts like a fence, and must be of much sturdier construction than the type of trellis designed to be fixed to a wall.

ABOVE: *Fencing in traditional materials has a rustic charm, enhanced by woodland climbers such as honeysuckle.*
LEFT: **Wisteria festooning trailed along a fence top is within easy reach for pruning. Its flowerheads are dense and compact.**

Though trellis makes a good boundary, you may want more privacy, particularly in winter when the leaves have fallen off the plants and the trellis itself becomes more apparent. A fence 1.5m (5ft) high with a length of trellis 50–60cm (20–24in) deep fixed along the top will give privacy while at the same time maintaining an open feel. The trellis allows climbers to get a firm hold and gives a colourful and softer line to the top of the fence.

TRELLIS

Because stems can weave in and out, and tendrils can grip around the wood, trellis is an ideal support for climbers. It is, therefore, a useful and convenient method of providing support on walls or fences. Fixing trellis to walls and fences offers another opportunity to experiment with colours. For example, brightly coloured trellis can have a startling effect against a white, or black, background. Try combining the colour of the background with that of the trellis and of the planting to create interesting harmonies or exciting contrasts; for example, dark blue trellis works well against a light blue background with the delicate pale violet flowers of *Codonopsis convolvulacea*.

Closely spaced trellis, used as panels or to give the impression of depth on a wall, is best left unplanted so that its architectural qualities can be enjoyed.

Trellis panels are available ready-made in a range of styles, but making your own is also relatively easy; it involves cutting lengths of wood and screwing or nailing them together. Hardwoods will last longer, but softwood treated with preservative is a good alternative and will last many years. There are no complicated joints to contend with. When building your own trellis, try to keep the thickness of the wood, the size of the squares and the overall size of the structure in visual proportion with each other. Panels of varied shapes and sizes can be made quite simply, and can be used to striking effect.

A trellis panel can be attached to a wall easily by means of screws. To make sure that there is room for the twining shoots to get behind the laths and attach themselves securely, bring the panel away from the wall with wooden spacers under the points where the trellis is screwed on.

On painted walls or wooden buildings that are going to need a preservative treatment, it pays to fix the trellis with hinges on its bottom edge and provide catches to hold the top in place. By undoing the catches, the whole panel with the plants still attached can be carefully angled away from the building for painting, leaving the plants completely unharmed.

LEFT: *The different colours of this trellis and Clematis 'Jackmanii' create a striking effect.*
RIGHT: *With very careful management, this astonishing screen of live willow shoots will last for several years.*

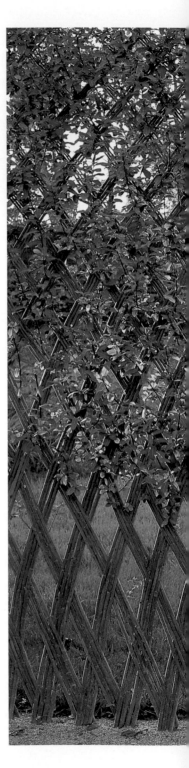

DIVISIONS AND 'SCREENS'

Any garden, however small, needs an element of mystery. There should be parts of the garden hidden from view, areas where the imagination is made to work, anticipating the surprise around the corner. Dividing up a small garden with solid walls or fences only helps to emphasize its smallness. By using more open screens or trellis, a feeling of intimacy can be created, while maintaining an airy feel by allowing glimpses through the partition to other parts of the garden. Such a garden is divided, but still succeeds in keeping its sense of space.

'Screen' is a term used generally to describe any vertical division within the garden that disguises unsightly objects or defines a garden 'room', and therefore includes internal fences and free-standing trellis. In an informal garden, short sections of fencing can be used to screen areas, adding twists and turns to pathways, creating secret corners to be discovered as you walk around the garden.

When viewed through free-standing trellis, each part of the garden can borrow something from the next – a single bloom framed in a trellis square, a scent carried through the open lattice, a flower on the trellis complementing the colour of a distant blossom, light dappled through the lattice highlighting blooms and deepening shadows. Trellis has the ability both to separate the garden and at the same time unite its elements.

The practical benefits of trellis, as compared with solid screens such as walls, are the extra light it allows through, which helps produce sturdier plants, and the greater air movement, which reduces the effect of harsh eddying winds.

A secluded area of the garden enclosed by trellis undergoes a change of character as the growing season progresses. The light and openness of early summer is gradually reduced as plants put on leaf, and new shoots fill the empty spaces. Views through are lost, and the wind is filtered to a gentle breeze by the ever more luxuriant foliage. A secret garden becomes more secret.

Other types of screen are simple to make for anyone who can use a hammer and a handsaw, or can simply tie a knot in a piece of rope. Within the garden you can find an assortment of potential materials suitable for screens – garden canes, willow prunings (for weaving), hazel sticks, vine prunings that can be plaited, and broken branches that can be worked into patterns. Outside the garden there is an even wider range of materials. Traditional wooden planking can be arranged in many ways – upright, at an angle, horizontally, or a mixture of all three. Metal piping, in copper, aluminium or steel, complements a modern garden or creates an incongruous focal point in a more traditional garden.

Rope is very versatile, and forms a loose screen when tied between two posts in horizontal rows. Coloured rope will add interest. Screens made of any of the above materials can be hung, hammock-style, from ropes between trees, or dropped from branches on vertical ropes like stage scenery. Try hanging rope in vertical rows from a single wooden beam, and attaching trinkets (such as coloured-glass bottles, pieces of pottery, shells, driftwood and old garden forks and trowels) to add colour and texture. Old ladders, laid on their side and supported by stakes at each end, make a novel but easily constructed screen.

PLANTING AGAINST SCREENS

It is easy to establish climbing plants against screens because, if they are of an open construction, plants will be able to weave in and out, removing the need for attaching them by means of wires or netting. The more elaborate a screen, the less planting is necessary. Fine detail will be smothered by over-vigorous plants, whereas more delicate plants let the intricacies show through; so be sure to choose complementary plants.

The character of each area within the garden can be enhanced by the choice of climbers used on the screen. A light, romantic feeling can be instilled using the pretty-leaved *Akebia quinata*,

ABOVE: *The greenery on the trellis and unglazed 'doors' gives the impression of a summer pavilion abandoned to nature.*

LEFT: *Harmonizing the colour of planting with screening unifies a garden. Here, the plants, container and trellis are all of a similar tone.*

with its 'hands' of rounded leaves and scented, purple flowers, and the small, dark green leaves of *Billardiera longiflora*. For a bolder, jungle-like effect, try juxtaposing the large leaves of the vigorous (but manageable) *Vitis coignetiae* with the peculiarly shaped flowers and light green, heart-shaped leaves of *Aristolochia macrophylla*.

PROJECT: *TRELLIS FANS*

THESE PAINTED fans not only complement the climbers grown on them but also look good during the winter months. A pattern of inverted, adjacent fans helps to break up large, uninteresting areas of wall or fence.

MATERIALS AND TOOLS

6 pieces of planed timber 1.2cm x 3.4cm
   (½in x 1¼in), 2.4m (8ft) long
Tape measure, handsaw and set square
Approx 35 2cm (1in) galvanized nails
4 x 5cm (2½in) screws and wall plugs
Primer, undercoat, blue paint and brush

PLANTS

Clematis montana
Lonicera x *brownii* 'Dropmore Scarlet'

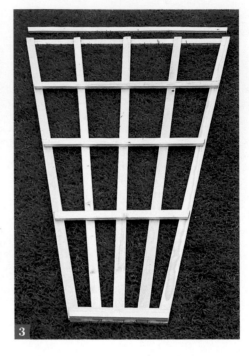

• Cut three pieces of wood 1.5m (5ft), 0.9m (3ft) and 0.3m (1ft) in length. Mark the centre point of the pieces measuring 0.9m and 0.3m. Working flat on the ground lay these pieces horizontally. Then lay the 1.5m piece at right angles (vertically) on the two centre points that you have marked. Check all is square (**1**) and secure this piece with two nails at each end.

• Lay the 2.4m sides and intermediate vertical pieces flush with the bottom horizontal and, using a pencil, mark where they meet along the top. Cut each to length and fix them with two nails at the top and the bottom (**2**).

• On the central vertical lath mark heights at the quarter, half and three-quarter points. Lay pieces of your remaining wood horizontally across at these points and mark their exact lengths. Cut the pieces accordingly and nail them on (**3**). These strips will provide extra rigidity and give the climbers more to cling on to.

• Prime and undercoat the wood before finishing with a coat of exterior paint. Drill two holes in both the top and bottom horizontals and, checking that it is level, screw the trellis fan to the fence. (Drill and plug if screwing the trellis to a wall.)

• Plant the climbers at the foot of the trellis and tie in trailing shoots with string. To prevent the string from slipping, tie it first round the trellis and then around the plant stem.

RIGHT: *The plants will take a little while to attach themselves and become firmly established on the trellis but it should make an attractive feature within the first year. The clematis and honeysuckle will grow vigorously and will soon achieve a decent coverage. Try using a number of trellis fans as well as different plant and paint colours to create a variety of exciting combinations.*

PROJECT: BALCONY PARTITION

MATERIALS AND TOOLS

Large, stout trough

Trellis panel

Gravel and soil-based compost

PLANTS

2 *Solanum jasminoides* 'Album'

2 *Rhodochiton atrosanguineus*

2 *Lathyrus odoratus* 'Matucana'

• Assemble the materials (**1**). Place the trough next to the trellis. Make sure that there are plenty of drainage holes in it

THOSE WITH ONLY a balcony or paved yard need not despair of growing climbers, as many can be grown easily in containers. Here trellising provides privacy and shelter on an exposed balcony. Balcony railings can be put to similar use. Attach large mesh netting to provide extra grip for finer plants.

and cover the bottom with a layer of gravel about 4cm (1½in) thick (**2**). Fill to within 2.5cm (1in) of the top with compost.

• Space the plants evenly along the length of the trough. Plant them in compost to the same depth as when in the pot (**3**). Water them in.

• The intimacy of a balcony allows flowers to be seen close up (**4**). In this way, the beauty of their colour, shape, texture and scent can be fully appreciated.

RIGHT: *Screening a balcony with plants ensures the vitality of greenery is just a step away from the living space.*

CLIMBING PLANTS can be grown on many different structures in the garden, creating features that are both beautiful and useful. Pergolas provide a shady spot for outdoor entertaining; arches mark entrances and frame views; tunnels make deliciously scented walkways and arbours are the perfect setting for romantic encounters. The basic structures can be as complex or as simple as you like, improvized from materials in the garden or purchased ready made. In all cases they will add interest to the garden providing architectural focal points, helping to define its style and moods, and increasing your scope for exploiting the fragrance, foliage and flowers of climbing plants.

Garden Structures

ABOVE: *Arches allow fleeting glimpses into other parts of the garden, so building up a feeling of anticipation.*
LEFT: *Densely planted arches create an intimacy in the garden that insulates anyone within from the outside world.*

PERGOLAS

A pergola is an open structure designed to carry plants above a path or terrace. Rows of uprights support an overhead lattice of wood. The sides may be kept open to create a shaded avenue, or smothered in growth, to direct the eye straight ahead towards a focal point.

A pergola can be very useful as a means of unifying awkward spaces around a building. Positioned directly against the house, it provides a shady, leafy area for sitting out. Viewed from behind French doors, it gives the effect of carrying the room through to the outdoors and, conversely, bringing the garden into the house.

An informal pergola can be constructed easily from two rows of closely spaced rustic poles dug into and positioned upright in the ground. The pairs of poles are each joined at the top with a horizontal pole that juts beyond the verticals. This simple idea can be suited to a more formal setting by using planed timber instead of rustic poles. Shape the protruding ends by cutting them at an angle or by rounding them off. Adapt the design further by running horizontal timbers across the pairs of poles and then resting crosspieces on them. This allows close spacing of the overhead beams for a more roofed-over effect. A rail or rope can be attached between the uprights to separate the walkway from the garden. Climbers can be trained along these too.

The pergola can be made more enclosed by filling the side spaces with trellis, either completely or to half the height. To create a 'roof', fix wires or trellis between widely spaced beams. Trellis is preferable, because it requires less tying in of plants, provides continuous support,

and is still attractive when the plants lose their leaves. Boxing in or making the 'pillars' out of trellis as well will create a sumptuous-looking pergola.

Pillars can also be built from brick or stone, or a layered combination of the two. This makes for substantial uprights which will need to be balanced by heavy timber crossbars. Wrought-iron pillars have a distinct character. Because of the strength of the iron, it is possible to make an open and airy-looking structure with a very different feel from the usual weighty construction. Be very careful, however, not to overplant and spoil the openness.

The main considerations when constructing a pergola are that the uprights are strong and well secured in the ground, and that the crosspieces will support the weight of the plants and, in certain areas, a thick covering of snow. Materials must be durable. Hardwoods are ideal, but pressure-treated softwoods will last many years.

Metal-tubing uprights are very strong, but are usually only suitable near the house, as they look out of place in all but the most architectural of gardens. Metal does take paint well, and for a lively effect use bright colours combined with garden furniture painted in cheerful primaries. Planting should then be kept simple, using strong green foliage as a foil for the bold background colours.

Make sure that the pergola is high enough, allowing sufficient space for people to walk underneath it comfortably even when it is smothered in foliage.

RIGHT: *Simple designs are often the best. A plain pergola planted with a white wisteria creates a clean, uncomplicated effect.*

PLANTS FOR PERGOLAS AND ARBOURS

Pergolas offer the opportunity for some bold planting effects with some of the showier climbing plants. One of the classic plantings is wisteria. Walking through curtains of scented lilac flowers hanging down in early summer is an experience not forgotten. Take the leading shoot up the pillar, removing or shortening any sideshoots. When it reaches the top, let it branch out across the top of the pergola. Tie new shoots in to the horizontal. When a framework of branches has formed, simply shorten the sideshoots after flowering.

Covered with scented plants, a pergola envelopes you in perfume. Roses that hold their flowers up on stiff stems will lose most of their effect on a pergola unless seen from above, so choose ramblers and roses that cascade (such as *Rosa* 'Crimson Shower' and the blush-pink *R.* 'Paul's Himalayan Musk'). Bundle the stems of rambling roses together around the uprights, and tie them with twine. In a fairly open pergola, run supporting wires at right angles to the beams and tie in the rose stems. With more closely spaced beams, or with timber running along the length as well as the width of the pergola, the shoots of the roses will rest across the top. From underneath, tuck back in any shoots that come through.

Plants will not find it easy to grip onto smooth wooden posts, so you will need to tie them on. Tie a length of string around the post and then around the plant. Alternatively, attach a screw-eye to the post and tie the plant to the eye. A textured surface that provides more grip can be created by wrapping the post spirally with flexible stems of willows. Rope is an easier, and perhaps more readily available, alternative.

ARBOURS

Arbours have a variety of uses in the garden. Typically, they are sited as focal points at the end of a walk or pergola, with larger arbours often used as shaded seating areas. The plants provide shade while the open sides allow a breeze to blow through. Larger arbours also make impressive features when located at the crossing-point of two paths. In smaller gardens, an arbour can be used to make an intimate garden room, big enough to hold a small table and chairs.

Styles of arbour range from large, elaborate, metalwork structures, used to form major focal points, to simple wooden benches under canopies. Such canopies might include seats placed into an overhanging recess cut in a hedge, or set beneath a roof made of trained branches. These can be created from hedging plants like beech, hornbeam or yew.

A construction made of wooden trellis panels requires only basic skills, but more elaborate designs can require specialist equipment, and are best built by a carpenter or bought ready-made.

A simple arbour can be built with unstripped, rustic logs. You will need two uprights at each side, joined across the top by horizontal pieces (running from front to back on each side). Two further pieces, spanning the width, complete the 'roof'. To make it rigid, fix pieces of wood across all the top corners to create triangles. Any crudeness of construction will be hidden as the plants grow. Make sure that there will be sufficient space beneath the

ABOVE: *An arbour can be painted to complement the colours of the garden in spring, before the growth of climbers obscures the framework.*
LEFT: *Lightweight, metal-framed arbours can look flimsy but once they are clad in climbers such as ivy, they become more substantial.*

arbour for you to sit comfortably once the grown plants hang through. More elaborate designs include creating an arched roof, using bowed wooden laths, or bringing the roof to a point.

There is little benefit in making an arbour too elaborate, particularly if that means extra maintenance. It is inconvenient to have to remove plants from metal and wooden arbours in need of regular painting. Avoid painting metalwork white, as it distracts the eye and soon looks shabby. Choose darker colours such as bottle-green or deep blue. Black is another option, and it looks pristine for longer than many other colours.

An arbour of tree stems can be made from long wands of *Populus alba*. In the dormant season, plant them in bundles of three in a semicircle and plait each group together. When the plaits have grown long enough, arch them over and tie them at the top. The stems will thicken and fuse to form a living, ribbed enclosure. Prune off any sideshoots to keep the arbour in shape.

TUNNELS

Tunnels create a special feeling. Walking down a cool, leafy tunnel, with dappled light filtering through, you are in a world of your own – a place of shady walkways and enchanting shadows.

When making or choosing a tunnel, ensure that it is high and wide enough to walk through after plants have been established. The size and shape of the tunnel will affect the feeling you get as you walk through it. The wider the walkway, the more you are encouraged to take your time and enjoy the experience. A bare frame may look big, but when it is covered in vegetation you will lose 30–45cm (12–18in) from the top of the arch and each of the sides. Be as bold with the length, width and height of the tunnel as you dare, but remember to keep it in proportion with the rest of the garden.

Tunnels also work well when pitched against a wall, the wall forming one side of the tunnel. Vines are ideal on a sunny wall, creating a shady walkway for a summer hot spot as well as providing a crop of grapes. For an exciting feature, install two tunnels that intersect at right angles, the point at which they join is the ideal spot for a garden sculpture or ornament.

Making an arched tunnel from wood requires bracing and supporting, but a triangular-shaped tunnel of wooden poles is both easy to construct and unusual. Poles 3m (10ft) in height will give reasonable clearance if just rested on the ground; if

RIGHT: *Sunlight filtering through the leaves, the coolness of the shade and the feeling of enclosure create a mysterious and magical atmosphere inside a living tunnel.*

they are to be set into the ground, add another 30–40cm (12–16in). Set at least two pairs into the ground to hold the frame firm. They can be nailed, drilled or bolted together, or simply bound together with cord. A horizontal pole joining the tops of the triangles will make the structure rigid.

Tunnels ready-made from plastic-coated steel can be purchased off the shelf. Steel is robust and makes a strong and durable structure. For a larger project, the frames used by growers for polythene tunnels are extremely strong, although you will have to decrease the spacing between the sections to get a reasonable density of supports and you will need to hold them together along the top with a horizontal tube for extra stability.

More unusual materials than wood or steel can make exciting and novel features in the garden. Blue plastic water pipe, 25–35mm (1–1⅓in) in diameter, can be shaped to form a colourful tunnel. It will need three supports running horizontally to hold it rigid. These can be pieces of pipe held together by plastic plumbing fittings, or simply lengths of pipe bound to the hoops of the tunnel with cord. A length of dowel knocked into the ends of each hoop will help secure them in the ground.

PLANTS FOR TUNNELS

Growing climbers over tunnels brings you into close contact with the plants. Flowers are at eye level, letting you appreciate their beauty and detail, and the calm air holds their scent. Fruits, such as grapes from vines, hang down temptingly; curtains of wisteria blooms excite the senses with their scent, softness and colour. Other plants suitable for growing over tunnels are cucumbers, gourds, *Apios americana* and the scented *Akebia quinata*.

The shady ground inside a tunnel is an ideal environment for ferns and woodland plants. In spring, before the canopy of leaves shades the ground, primroses (*Primula vulgaris*), hellebores and snowdrops will thrive, gradually fading away as the leaves above cut out the sunshine.

In a less formal part of the garden, a living tunnel can be created by planting two rows of lime or hazel trees. As these grow up, arch them over until they touch. Initially this will take quite a lot of wiring in and training, but once the main branches have thickened they will stay in place and can be used as supports for tying in the younger shoots. As the trees grow and the trunks thicken, a ribbed wall of twisted branches develops, creating a mysterious atmosphere when viewed in evening light. Willow stems can also be used for a living tunnel.

ABOVE : *An imaginative use of garden flowers* (**Nicotiana langsdorfii** *and* **N. sylvestris**), *runner beans and supports gleaned from the garden itself gives this plot a practical but artistic look.*

ARCHES

Arches laden with scented blooms draw you through to explore the garden beyond. Like doorways, they guide you towards the garden rooms, but they do not close behind you; a glance back provides a framed view and a new angle on the room you have just left. Arches themselves can also form a focal point, bowed over an ornament or seat at the end of a pathway.

Timber is an ideal medium for arches, because it is easily worked and fastened together. Use it in the form of rustic poles, or in square-sawn or plank

form. Timber takes paint and woodstain, or it can be left in its natural state. The use of timber gives considerable scope when making an arch.

An arch with sides and a 'roof' made of flat planking gives the feeling of a formal doorway, particularly if stained or painted. Rough and rustic wood, on the other hand, has a more natural appearance, and looks as if it has grown up with the plants that cover it.

Arches made from willow branches create natural-looking openings in hedges, and provide good support for climbers. Long shoots cut in winter and pushed into the ground to form the sides of the arch may root and put out shoots in the spring. Form these shoots into an arch, tying them together until they thicken and hold their form. A quite severe annual pruning in winter will help keep the arch in good shape.

Long lengths of vine prunings can be bundled and tied together to form stiff 'ropes' that can be bent to form a simple arch, with each end tied to a short stake in the ground. The 'ropes' are quite rigid and self-supporting. Alternatively, a simple structure can be created from two large 'A'-frames joined along the top by a crossbeam. Arches can also be made from trellis.

PLANTS FOR ARCHES

Rambling roses and honeysuckles are ideal for growing over arches, as are *Trachelospermum jasminoides* and *Aristolochia macrophylla*.

LEFT: *In keeping with this cottage garden, an informal arch has been constructed from fallen branches bound with twine. The structure supports a leafy morning glory.*

PROJECT: *SECLUDED ARBOUR*

THIS PROJECT PROVIDES a protected sitting area surrounded by a curtain of hanging foliage and flowers. Quite severe pruning each spring will keep the vigorous vine within bounds.

MATERIALS AND TOOLS

4 pressure-treated wooden posts 10cm (4in) square, 2.6m (8ft 6in) long
Drill and bit (4cm/1½in) diameter
Fork, spade and sledgehammer
Spirit level and long straight-edge
4 post caps
Rope 6m (20ft) long, 4cm (1½in) diameter
Porous mulching fabric or black polythene, 2.3 x 1.7m (7ft 6in x 5ft 6in)
75 frostproof bricks
Gravel, about 0.25m^3 (2¾cu.ft)

PLANTS

4 *Fallopia baldschuanica*

• Mark the positions of the posts on the ground. The two front posts are 2.5m (8ft) apart and the back two 1.8m (6ft) apart. Mark these out from a centre line to ensure symmetry. The front-to-back measurement is 1.5m (5ft). Drill a hole, 5cm (2in) in diameter, through the top of each post, 10cm (4in) from the end (**1**). Dig four post holes 60cm (2ft) deep and set the posts in position. Check the tops are level with each other using a straight-edge and spirit level. Adding a few centimetres at a time, pound the soil in securely around each post with a sledge-hammer. Check the posts are upright (**2**) as the hole is filled. Nail on the post caps.

• Thread the rope through the holes, allowing it to sag evenly between the posts. Knot each end (**3**).

• Mark out the base and dig down to about 8cm (3in). Lay out the mulching fabric or plastic. If using plastic, poke some drainage holes into it. Edge the base with a row of bricks, end-to-end along the front and side-by-side around the edges. Fill in with gravel (**4**). Trim off excess sheeting.

• Dig the planting holes a little way from the posts. Position the plants so that they lean into the posts (**5**) and fill in around them. Tie the stems to the posts and encourage leading shoots along the rope.

RIGHT: *The mile-a-minute vine will quickly establish itself and produce a living curtain of foliage and flowers.*

PROJECT: VEGETABLE IGLOO

Measure out a 1.5m (5ft) square and push a piece of dowelling into the ground at each corner, leaving a quarter of each length sticking out. Push in the other two pieces at the midpoint of two opposite sides. Fit the two ends of the 3m (10ft) pipe over these two midpoint pieces (**2**). Fit the two longer pieces diagonally across the square.

• Where they cross, bind the three pipes tightly together with the nylon rope (**3**).

• After the last frost, plant a runner bean and a tomato plant at the base of each pipe. Tie in the beans until they start to twine. Tie in the tomatoes as they grow (**4**).

RIGHT: *Finding a second use for this old water pipe has provided a splash of colour and satisfied the recycling spirit of the allotment gardener.*

USING BRIGHT, DURABLE materials, this project makes a lively structure for supporting runner beans and tomatoes. It could also be used to grow sweet peas and clematis in the border.

MATERIALS AND TOOLS
Blue plastic water pipe 3cm (1¼in)
    diameter, 10m (33ft) long
Dowelling to the diameter of the piping,
cut into 6 x 40 cm (16in) lengths
Tape measure and saw
Blue nylon rope 1m (3ft) long
PLANTS
6 'Painted Lady' runner beans
6 'Gardener's Delight' tomato plants

• Prepare an open site with fertile, moisture-retentive soil (**1**).

• Cut two pieces of pipe 3.5m (11ft 6in) long and one piece 3m (10ft) long.

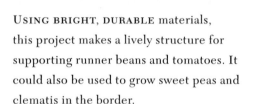

Various kinds of free-standing objects and structures can be used in the garden, draped with climbers, to create arresting focal points. These might include obelisks, pyramids and tripods – as well as other homemade, three-dimensional shapes – you are limited only by your imagination and the style and size of your garden. Brightly painted ornaments in the garden offer a chance to create bold and original designs, making imaginative use of colour. Wooden structures are easy to create and no special woodworking skills are needed. A trip to an architectural salvage yard or scrap-metal dealer will invariably prove fruitful hunting grounds for those with an adventurous outlook.

Ornamental Supports

ABOVE: *Ornamental ironwork is durable and, with a coat of paint, can be made to suit any colour scheme.*
LEFT: *A thicket of upright canes creates a striking feature, with a mixture of morning glories twisting their way up towards the light.*

Pyramids and Obelisks

Pyramids and obelisks have a place in both the formal and informal garden. In a formal garden, planting can be kept spare to emphasize structure. Use them in combination with neatly trimmed shapes and hedges. In an informal garden, they can be covered with plants to soften the rigid outlines.

Placing pyramids or obelisks at regular intervals along a path or a hedge will, if you are standing at one end, draw your attention along the row to a vista or focal point. Evenly spaced in a border, they provide structure and support. When positioned together as 'gateposts', obelisks can also be used to frame a view, or the entrance to a garden room. To increase the range of plants that you can grow in them, try standing pyramids on Versaille planters.

Pyramids and obelisks can be made from metal or wood, but metal structures need to be sufficiently heavy-gauge not to appear lightweight. They become almost invisible among the plants if painted in dark colours, and any starkness of form is quickly lost as the plants take over. Wooden supports are more obvious structures, because of the thickness of material required, but they will also weather well (as long as they are made from pressure-treated wood).

FAR LEFT: *Inconspicuous supports can add discreet structure to a border. This obelisk does not detract from the white colour scheme.*
LEFT: *The choice of more substantial supports is as important as the plants that clothe them, especially in winter when their outline is visible.*
RIGHT: *Elaborate tripods and obelisks give a sumptuous style to a garden, further enhanced by plantings of* Clematis 'Etoile Violette' *and* Lathyrus odoratus 'Noel Sutton'.

A simple wooden obelisk is easy to construct. A 20cm- (8in-) square piece of wood, about 4cm (1½in) thick, forms the top, to which uprights are attached. A 40cm- (16in-) square piece of wood forms a support platform attached towards the bottom of the uprights, about 20cm (8in) from their ends. Four pieces of 3 × 1cm (1½ × ½in) wood, 2m (6½ft) long, form the uprights. Using screws or nails, attach the ends of the uprights to each corner of the top square. Splay them out and nail each one to the other squares, positioning it as described.

Fill in between the uprights with a diagonal latticework of 3 × 1cm (1½ × ½in) strips; or, for a plainer effect, use strips vertically, held together with two or three horizontal crosspieces. Ornamental shapes can then be placed on the top.

COLOUR SCHEMES

Obelisks and pyramids are prominent structures, and if painted, they can be made to have even more impact. Balance the colour of the structure with that of the planting. While dark green is less obtrusive than lighter colours and allows the plants to take the spotlight, brighter colours, such as yellow or pink, for example, vie with flowers and

foliage. A warm orange works well with *Kniphofia* 'Atlanta' or *K.* 'Royal Standard', and later with crocosmias and rudbeckias. Cool the scheme with *Anthemis tinctoria* 'E.C. Buxton'. If a border has a colour theme, then unify the scheme by choosing a complementary colour for the obelisk. Alternatively, a contrasting colour will make it stand out.

Avoid white, because it dirties easily and distracts the eye. Instead, a mustard yellow provides an interesting contrast to the vibrant red of *Rosa* 'Danse du Feu' or the blackish-red flowers of *R.* 'Guinée', and, for the late season, the violet flowers of *Clematis* 'Etoile Violette', from the *viticella* group. For a harmonious effect try 'muddy' blue paintwork with *C.* 'Elvan', another *viticella* group clematis, which has hanging, purple flowers. The advantage of the *viticella* and *texensis* groups of clematis is that they have fine leaves and flowers, and are less likely to overwhelm the structure.

If you find choosing colours difficult, look for inspiration elsewhere: in magazines, other people's gardens or shop-windows. Even if you use just three types of climber – clematis, roses and sweet peas, for example – you can have attractive colour throughout the seasons.

To give your garden an instant facelift, just repaint the pyramid or obelisk. Using two colours on an obelisk – one on the main framework, another on the rest – means that you can choose plants that complement each colour. For example, try a primrose-yellow and buttercup-yellow for the obelisk, together with the yellow to orange-yellow flowers of the marmalade bush.

When choosing flower colours, do not rely on photographs in books. It is better to match your flower colour against a sample of painted wood.

ABOVE: *The simplest garden tripod is constructed using three garden canes bound together with string or wire at the top.*

TRIPODS

A tripod consists of three poles leant together and fastened at the top. Easy to construct, they are made from lightweight canes for annuals and heavy-duty poles for more robust plants. They take up little room, and are ideal for small plots or potagers.

The simplest form is made of garden canes, and is the type usually seen supporting runner beans, but it can be used in a border to support the cup-and-saucer plant (*Cobaea scandens*), sweet peas and climbing nasturtiums. Wrap the tripod in black or green large-mesh nylon netting, so that the

plants can get a better grip and are less likely to be blown off. They will soon mask the netting.

On a larger scale, use wooden posts 8–10cm (3–4in) in diameter. Arrange them as a tripod and bind them with rope. Secure the base 30cm (1ft) into the ground for stability. Tall tripods are ideal for climbing and rambling roses. Wrap the stems around the tripod to encourage shoots to sprout all along the stem. This results in a denser covering and a greater number of flowers.

LEFT: *Natural materials are perfect for an informal garden. These hazel poles provide support for sweet peas.*
BELOW: *A tripod of wood with cross-strings provides a sturdy and appealing support.*

Alternative materials include hazel branches. These are unobtrusive and provide a good rough surface for plants to climb around. If hazel is not available, any long straight shoots or branches will do as, when used for annuals, they only need to last one season. Broom handles offer a middle-weight alternative to garden canes and heavy-duty poles.

For a modern look, try using copper piping. This can be painted, left to weather, or cleaned to a bright finish with wire wool, then coated with a clear polyurethane varnish to keep it sparkling. It can be bound at the top with copper wire stripped from old electrical cable. This smooth surface will be best suited to plants that climb by twining; self-clinging plants will find it hard to grip. This style of tripod would suit an 'architectural' garden, but could also stand out as a quirky contrast in a cottage-garden setting. The colour of the copper may be slightly difficult to match with plants. Try *Lonicera × heckrottii*, with its pink and orange flowers, or the dusty purple of *Clematis viticella* 'Purpurea Plena Elegans'. The clematis may need tying on until it gets established. A tangle of woody prunings inside the tripod will provide a base for the young shoots to get a hold of.

IMPROVIZED SUPPORTS

To add some originality to your garden, think about improvizing plant supports. This might mean using natural materials found within the confines of the garden itself, although looking outside the garden for manmade items may prove just as successful.

LEFT: *Rope provides a good surface for twining and clinging plants such as* Humulus lupulus *'Aureus' or* Fallopia baldschuanica.

NATURAL MATERIALS

Plant prunings, such as vine stems, make good improvised supports. Cut these out in winter, keeping them as long as possible and leaving the tendrils on for character and extra grip. Tie them in bundles of six or more, and attach them to a wall using vine-eyes and wire. Because the vines are flexible, they can be bent into curved shapes.

You can create fine braids by plaiting shoots of wisteria when they are cut out in late summer. For an even more durable framework, plait three of these braids together. The braids can be looped over a pot to hold light climbers like sweet peas and longer lengths can be used in the borders. Form them into shapes while they are still green and pliable.

Willow wands are probably the most versatile garden by-product. Professionally made designs, such as old fish traps and simple tubes, can be bought, and make excellent supports. It is not difficult, however, to produce homemade versions. For long vigorous shoots, cut willows hard back every year or two, in spring. This also encourages the plant to produce colourful stems. *Salix alba* cultivars, S. *daphnoides* and S. *purpurea* are all suitable for this purpose.

Collect stems of approximately equal length and diameter. To make a 'fish-trap' support, push the thick end of the stems into the ground, 10–12cm (4–5in) apart, in a circle. Tie the tops together to form a wigwam. Weave in thinner stems, starting at the base, until you have completed five or six circles. Repeat this three or more times at intervals up the framework. These horizontal bindings hold the structure together. It can now be removed from the ground and placed where desired.

ABOVE: *A natural support made from willow wands is particularly appropriate in a cottage-garden setting.*

If using dormant stems cut during the winter, there is a chance that if left in the ground they will root. This can produce a leafy, natural-looking plant support that will need to be trimmed hard every year. It is best used as a short-term structure, however, and removed after two or three years; if left, it will become a multi-stemmed tree.

To prevent the stems from rooting, keep the framework out of the ground until the stems have died, or peel off the bark to above ground level. Small versions of this structure can be placed in pots and other containers.

To make a screen, push willow wands into the ground in a row, angling them alternately one way and then the other, to produce an attractive diamond pattern. If desired, this temporary structure can also be left to take root.

MANMADE MATERIALS

A simple wooden screen – made of two uprights, 2m (6ft) high and 2m (6ft) apart, joined by four or five horizontal wooden rails – is ideal for growing climbing roses in a border. For a 'solid wall' of flowers and foliage in the summer, weave the stems through the horizontals.

An upright trellis column, 40–50cm (16–20in) square and 2m (6ft) high, can be made from trellis panels, and used to support climbers like clematis. Eventually, the structure will be hidden by plants.

To create a more elegant tripod-like support, place a 2.5–3m- (8–10ft-) long, 8cm- (3in-) diameter pole in the ground. Take four pieces of rope or chain and attach one end of each to the top of the pole. Trail the other end 1m (3ft) from the pole and peg it securely into the ground.

Old ladders, positioned against a fence or wall or stood back-to-back, are useful in the vegetable garden as supports, or in the ornamental garden as an alternative to obelisks. Wooden ladders are more natural; aluminium ladders benefit from a coat of paint. Self-supporting stepladders can also be used.

An old rotary washing line can be used as a support for rambling roses such as *Rosa* 'Paul Transon' – trained up and over, this leafy plant with salmon-pink flowers makes a large 'standard' rose.

Some antique iron bedsteads sport elegant finials and elaborate scrolls; used in a fence in an informal setting, such a bedhead would give a fanciful effect. Ensure, however, that you do not overplant them, or the effect will be lost.

LEFT: *An old window frame supports the flowers of Clematis 'Alba Luxurians', which weave their way through the missing panes.*

In an orchard, climbing plants can be laced along ropes between trees. This method can also be employed between trees in an avenue. Use plants that develop a permanent framework from which flowers are produced, such as wisteria and climbing roses.

Almost anything lends itself as a support to ivy. An annual clipping will encourage the ivy to take on the shape of the object it is covering. For a touch of humour, cover a table and chairs. When grown up a post, ivy can stand in for a narrow conifer.

PROJECT: *ABANDONED LADDER*

MATERIALS AND TOOLS
Old stepladder
Dark green paint
PLANTS
Lonicera x *heckrottii*
Humulus lupulus 'Aureus'
Clematis 'Duchess of Albany'
Solanum crispum 'Glasnevin'

• Assemble the materials and plants (**1**). After removing all the dirt and dust from the ladder, paint it, priming and under-coating if necessary, (**2**).

• For each of the four selected plants, dig a hole in a position slightly away from the side of one of the legs of the ladder. Before planting, incorporate a little general fertilizer into the soil that has been removed from the hole.

• Place each plant in a hole, so that it is leaning towards the ladder. Fill in around the plant with the fertilized soil, firm the plant in, and spread any excess soil around it on the surface. Water the plants in thoroughly.

A REDUNDANT WOODEN stepladder provides solid support for a colourful mix of climbers. Here juniper-green paint shows off a lime-green hop, pink-flowering clematis and honeysuckle, and a blue-flowering solanum. A bright colour could be used to harmonize with a primary-colour-themed planting. Painted aluminium steps can also be effective.

and allow it to dry. Place the ladder in the garden where there is soft soil. Try a variety of different angles and positions until you are satisfied with how it looks in relation to buildings or existing features.

• Stand on the first step to push the legs as far into the ground as possible. Repeat on the other side until the ladder is level.

• Loosely tie the plants to a leg of the ladder until they start to attach themselves as they grow (**3**). The solanum will need extra tying to attach itself.

RIGHT: *A mixture of intertwining hop, clematis, honeysuckle and solanum creates an abundance of growth by the end of the season.*

PROJECT: *SKIRTED SCARECROW*

HERE IS A PROJECT designed to scare the crows and cheer up the vegetable garden. It will also provide some nasturtium flowers to brighten up a salad.

MATERIALS AND TOOLS

9 garden canes, 2.1m (7ft) long

12 garden canes, 1.2m (4ft) long

Strong string and raffia

Strips of sacking, 7.5cm (3in) wide

Shallow terracotta pot

PLANTS

4 nasturtium plants, or 8 seeds

• Assemble the materials (**1**). Push the long canes into the ground, making a circle about 75cm (2ft 6in) in diameter (**2**).

• Gather the canes together and tie them tightly with string, about 40cm (16in) from the top (**3**).

• Tie the short canes together, 20cm (8in) from one end, using a strip of sacking. Split the other end into two roughly equal bundles and pass one in front of and one behind the upright canes. Tie these loose ends together with another piece of sacking. This should be enough to hold the arms in position while you also tie them tightly in the middle (**4**).

• Push the raffia on to the top of the upright canes and place the pot upside-down on top. Plant the four nasturtiums around the inside of the circle of canes, or push two seeds into the ground at the base of four of the canes. When the shoots are long enough, tie them to the canes to encourage them to climb.

RIGHT: *A touch of humour is always welcome in the garden and will not look out of place in a vegetable patch.*

PROJECT: *IVY STAR*

USING SIMPLE MATERIALS, this project creates a portable living ornament. Other shapes, like circles or diamonds are just as easily fashioned.

MATERIALS AND TOOLS
Wire, 3mm (⅛in) diameter, 2.4m (8ft) long
String, pliers and tape measure
Waterproof sticky tape
Flower pot, 25cm (10in) diameter
Compost
PLANTS
2 *Hedera helix* 'Light Fingers'

• Assemble the materials and soak the plants (**1**). With pliers, grip the wire 25cm (10in) from one end and bend to an angle of 70–80 degrees (**2**). Measure

13cm (5in) further along and bend it back to start a zigzag pattern. Repeat this until there are 15 bends. Bring the two straight ends together to make a pronged base for the star. Tape them together (**3**). Adjust the wire to make the star an even shape.

• Fill the pot with compost and push in the wire prong. Plant the ivies at the foot of the star and tie the trailing stems to the wire (**4**). As the ivies grow, keep tying in the leading shoots and cutting off any wayward sideshoots.

RIGHT: *Evergreen shapes are useful to give structure to a collection of flowering pot plants. In winter they can be the mainstay of a patio planting.*

MANY CULTIVATED CLIMBERS originate from wild species whose only means of support are other, more robust plants such as trees and shrubs. With a little imagination, you can make use of these natural supports to create unusual features and plant associations in your garden.

Established trees make ideal supports for vigorous climbers such as *Vitis coignetiae* or *Rosa mulliganii*, which could smother lesser plants. On a smaller scale, garden shrubs will provide an interesting frame for less vigorous climbers. No tying or training is needed once the climber is established, as the shrub provides twigs and branches to cling to. Flower colours and leaf textures can be contrasted with the host plant.

Living Supports

ABOVE: *Fruit trees past their prime make good hosts for vigorous climbing roses like* **Rosa heleniae**.

LEFT: *A plain yew hedge is brought to life by the trails of brilliant red flowers of* **Tropaeolum speciosum** *– a hardy climber* .

DESIGN AND PRACTICALITIES

When pairing a climber with a host plant, you must consider time of flowering, colour and vigour, as well as growing and pruning requirements. Use a climber that will not be in full flower when the host plant needs pruning. For example, spring-flowering shrubs usually need pruning straight after flowering, so combine these with summer- or autumn-flowering climbers. The aspect, temperature and soil requirements of both plants need to be the same.

The planting hole for the climber should be dug as large as possible, and filled with moisture-retentive organic matter, as well as some general fertilizer. For the first two or three seasons, until the climber is established, water and check regularly, and drive a spade down around the edge of the planting hole to cut off any invading roots.

CLIMBERS IN TREES

Climbers allowed to grow unchecked into trees can produce dramatic results. In autumn, the fiery leaves of *Vitis coignetiae* in the topmost branches of a mature tree are a wonderful sight, as are the sprays of perfumed flowers produced by *Rosa mulliganii*.

However, as grand as these spectacles are, a compromise has to be reached if you want your tree and climber to co-exist. Rampant climbers like *Rosa filipes* 'Kiftsgate', which is often recommended for hiding ugly sheds, will completely smother an apple tree, and then your garage and house if you are not careful. Choose suitable climbers, or be prepared to do some regular, merciless pruning.

The vigour of the climber needs to match the structure of the tree. Evergreens such as holly (*Ilex*) and yew (*Taxus baccata*) make the best backgrounds, particularly for climbing roses. Trees with brittle branches, such as robinias, should be avoided. Also remember to bear in mind the natural stature of a tree and do not spoil it unnecessarily with the distraction of a climber.

LEFT: *The majestic scale of large and vigorous climbers established in mature trees leads to a rich diversity of light, shade and colour.*

RIGHT: *Allowing climbing plants to find their own way through the trees will create a garden that both looks and feels relaxed and unforced.*

For large trees, try wisteria, *Clematis montana* or *Vitis coignetiae*. For smaller trees, such as old fruit trees, try *Clematis flammula* or *C. armandii*. The hermaphrodite *Celastrus orbiculatus*, with its butter-yellow leaves and orange seeds in autumn, looks beautiful hanging out of a tall evergreen; while the bright yellow flowerheads of *Lonicera* × *tellmanniana* and *L. tragophylla* make a brilliant show through dark evergreen foliage.

Self-clinging climbers like *Hydrangea anomala petiolaris* and parthenocissus are very useful for covering bare trunks. They need less tying in and the ascending stems add texture to the tree trunk.

ESTABLISHING CLIMBERS IN TREES

Under a tree, the ground is very dry and shady, and climbers may only have a bare trunk to cling to. Little can be done about shady conditions, other than planting on the sunny side of the tree in the hope of catching as much light as possible. Dryness, however, can be partially overcome by planting the climber a short distance (usually about 1–1.2m/ 3–4ft) away from the base of the tree. To avoid tree roots, all climbers should be planted at least 0.75m (2½ft) from the base. Trees vary in their rooting habits. Some, such as cherries and yews, have roots that lie near the surface, and the roots of climbers will compete with these. Other trees have roots that go straight down; these are easier to deal with.

If the climber is planted away from the tree, you will have to lean a cane between the base of the climber and the tree, securing it at both ends. Once the climber has grown along the cane, the stems will need to be tied with string to the trunk and branches until established. If the climber is planted near low branches, it can be started by means of

LEFT: **Humulus lupulus *'Aureus' grows through the shrub* Picea pungens 'Koster'.**
RIGHT: **Here Choisya ternata 'Sundance' supports a necklace of Tropaeolum tuberosum.**

ropes trailing from the branches to the ground. However, this can only be done successfully with plants like honeysuckle that are strong enough to withstand the movement of branches in the wind.

CLIMBERS IN SHRUBS

Most shrubs have a single flowering period, but those with colourful stems and bold foliage can hold their own even when out of flower. Shrubs with less distinct foliage, such as philadelphus, make ideal supports for climbers that flower at a different time.

Good foliage shrubs with poor flowers, such as aucuba, are given a lift when combined with climbers like the passion flower (*Passiflora caerulea*). The dense foliage of the aucuba protects the passion flower, which produces exotic blooms throughout the second half of the season. Cut it hard back each year to prevent it smothering the host shrub.

Annual climbers such as sweet peas and *Ipomoea tricolor* can be grown through shrubs, then removed once they have flowered. Similarly, tender perennials with a scrambling habit can be used as annuals: planted among shrubs and left until the frosts finally take them.

Bidens ferulifolia can be treated in this way. Its fine shoots will scramble through shrubs and strong perennials, to bear yellow flowers. Another good

LEFT: *Passion flowers borrow the foliage of* **Lonicera nitida 'Baggesen's Gold'.**

RIGHT: *A harmonious combination of* **Viburnum plicatum 'Lanarth' and Clematis montana.**

climber is the felty-leaved *Helichrysum petiolare*. Often seen in hanging baskets, it displays unusual vigour (reaching a height of 2m/6ft) when planted in a border with a sturdy shrub to lean on.

Other suitable tender plants include some of the more vigorous *Pelargonium* cultivars such as *P.* 'Chocolate Peppermint' and *P.* 'Atomic Snowflake'. These are strong scramblers with large, colourful leaves that can be used to enhance a foliage scheme. Let them scramble over hostas or through the larger daylilies (*Hemerocallis*).

There are a few perennial climbers that die back, or can be cut back, each season. Because they do not build up into a mass of tangled stems, they neither smother the host nor need regular pruning. These include *Tropaeolum speciosum* and *T. tuberosum*, both of which have showy flowers and attractive leaves; and the less showy, late-flowering climbing monkshood (*Aconitum hemsleyanum*).

Shrubs can be used to support a limited range of vegetable crops. Climbing beans have considerable ornamental value, with flowers in white, red or purple. Alternatively, try growing bush-type tomatoes. They need plenty of water and a sunny position, but a twiggy shrub will provide ideal support. With both tomatoes and beans, you will need access for harvesting.

Some shrubs, such as ceanothus and fremonto-dendron, grow and flower particularly well against a wall, due to the warmth and protection it affords. Using walls as supports for such shrubs, therefore, will create an opportunity for fine colour combinations. Clematis offer a range of colours, from pink to purple and cream to lavender-blue, and a season of flowering from spring to late summer, that make them ideal for this purpose. All of these will go with the early, rich blue flowers of ceanothus. The vibrant blue of *Ceanothus* 'Italian Skies' is

particularly eye-catching when softened by the lilac-rose and deep pink of *Clematis* 'Nelly Moser'. Meanwhile, the dullish leaves of *Garrya elliptica* form a good backdrop for the late-season, lemon flowers of *Clematis* 'Bill MacKenzie'. Cut the clematis back in the winter to show off the long, grey-green catkins of the garrya.

CLIMBERS IN HEDGES

Hedges provide good background for borders, making a solid, textured backdrop. The range of foliage types, from the fine and furry clipped yew, to the bold and glossy leaves of the cherry laurel (*Prunus laurocerasus*), give a superb choice of effects when designing a garden.

Hedges can also be used as living supports for climbing plants. They do, however, have one or two drawbacks. They take a considerable amount of moisture and nutrition out of the soil, and this is an important consideration if they are to support climbers. They also need to be clipped regularly to keep them trim, and this can be damaging to plants climbing through and over them. To overcome this problem, it is necessary to understand the cutting requirements of different hedges. Deciduous hedges can be cut at any time during their dormant season. However, as a general rule, it is best not to cut evergreen hedges during winter when cold weather may cause damage. The ideal time to cut evergreen hedges is in fact late summer or early autumn – just the time when many climbers are in full flower. Therefore, you

LEFT: **Clematis 'Etoile Rose' has a delicacy of leaf and flower that stops it from overwhelming the foliage of the smoke bush (Cotinus coggygria).**

should choose plants like *Clematis alpina* and *C. macropetala* that flower early and tolerate being cut back later on. Old, established hedges may not be so vigorous as to need clipping each year, which means any of the annual climbers can be grown through them without concern. Leaving the hedge-cutting until late autumn enables you to enjoy the best of the late-summer flowers, and still have a tidy hedge. Delaying the clipping of yew lets you appreciate the full beauty of, for example, the flowers and blue berries of a *Tropaeolum speciosum* scrambling up through it. *Jasminum officinale*, a scented climber with white flowers in late summer, is another plant for which it is well worth delaying your hedge-clipping.

Deciduous hedges such as hawthorn, beech, hornbeam and berberis are much easier to manage. Deciduous climbers such as vitis and ampelopsis, or the herbaceous golden hop (*Humulus lupulus* 'Aureus'), can all be cut back with the hedge in winter. Annuals can be planted early and left to grow to maturity.

Another option, if you have the space, is simply to let the hedge grow unclipped for two or three years and then start again, cutting it back fairly hard, together with the climber. Most rambling roses will respond to this treatment and grow back up with the hedge. You may need to be extra harsh on the rose to ensure vigour in the first season after cutting back and to give the hedge a chance. The robust cherry laurel is also vigorous enough to cope with this treatment. On a smaller scale, use *Clematis* 'Etoile Violette' against the attractive yellow-green of *Lonicera nitida* 'Baggesen's Gold'. Both plants stand hard cutting back.

ABOVE: ***Golden privet (*Ligustrum ovalifolium 'Aureum'*) is given a sprinkling of spring colour by* Clematis macropetala.**

Large internal hedges of × *Cupressocyparis leylandii* look wonderful with huge hanging displays of roses. Try the rose-pink *Rosa* 'Climbing Madame Caroline Testout' for a summer and late-autumn show; or the yellow cluster-flowered *R*. 'Claire Jacquier' and freshly scented *R*. 'Albéric Barbier'.

PROJECT: WILLOW SCREEN

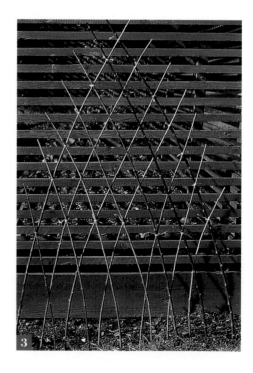

20cm (8in) from the top. From the left, push in six stems, 15cm (6in) apart, and tie them to the right-hand upright (**2**). Trim with secateurs.

• Repeat this process from the right, pushing the stems into the ground in between those already there. Cross them in front, and tie them to the stem furthest to the left (**3**). Plant a clematis 20cm (8in) in from each end. After the frosts, plant the lophospermum between the clematis.

RIGHT: ***The criss-cross of the willow wands and the tangles of foliage help soften the appearance of the fencing.***

will have roots and fresh, leafy shoots. Cut these back when they get too long.

MATERIALS AND TOOLS
14 willow stems 1.2m–1.8m (4–6ft) long
String
PLANTS
Clematis flammula
Clematis 'Madame Julia Correvon'
Lophospermum erubescens

• Choose an open sunny site and gather together the willow wands and plants (**1**).

• Push the two longest stems into the ground, about 1m (3ft) apart. Bend the tops together and tie with string about

THIS LIVING SCREEN can be shown off against a contrasting background or used as a free-standing divider in the garden. A mix of hardy and half-hardy plants gives a long succession of flowers. The willow stems are cut and planted during their winter dormancy. By spring they

When choosing which climbers to grow, consider their suitability both to complement and cover garden structures and as part of a planting scheme. Think about colour and shape – of leaves and flowers – and the species' growing habit. Think also about flowering season, hardiness and, of course, height. The following selection includes old favourites, such as rambling roses, ivies, honeysuckles and clematis, as well as some more unusual plants.

KEY TO SYMBOLS

❄ Hardy	☁ Shade
❅ Half-hardy	TW Twiner
⌂ Tender	SC Self-clinger
☀ Sun	EG Evergreen
⛅ Partial shade	

Plant Directory

ABOVE: *Given full sun, morning glory provides a spectacular succession of bell-shaped flowers in colours from deepest blue to red.*

LEFT: *The elegant Asarina purpusii has fine stems that thread their way through shrubs or trellis to hold aloft its opulent, yet delicate, flowerheads.*

ACONITUM HEMSLEYANUM (SYN. A. VOLUBILE)

This herbaceous, climbing monkshood will push through shrubs or perennials and produce clusters of hooded, lilac-mauve flowers in late summer. The plant dies down at the end of the season. **2–3m (6½–10ft).**
✽ ☼ ☁ TW

ACTINIDIA

A. deliciosa (Chinese gooseberry, kiwi fruit) is a fast-growing, deciduous twiner. The large leaves, with hairy undersides, are carried on robust stems covered in red hairs. Male and female flowers are usually borne on separate plants, but a hermaphrodite form is now available. Cut back side shoots to 15–23cm (6–9in) in late summer, and then again to one or two buds in early winter if growing for fruit. **12–15m (40–50ft).**

A. kolomikta grows more steadily, producing variegated leaves in green, pink and white. Full sun is needed to develop leaf colour (which improves as the plant ages). Grow it through a copper-beech hedge or on a pergola with pink clematis. **4.5m (15ft).**
✽ ☼ TW

AKEBIA QUINATA

A deciduous or semi-evergreen twiner. In spring it bears small, reddish-purple flowers that are best appreciated on a pergola or an arch. Each elegant leaf has five splayed lobes. The flowers, often hidden by the foliage, are betrayed by their scent. The plant produces sausage-like purple fruits, particularly if grown in a sheltered spot. **8–10m (25–35ft).**
✽ ☼ ☁ TW

AMPELOPSIS

A genus of vigorous, deciduous climbers that need space to grow well. They can be grown into a tree, over a building, or up a post. The growth should be kept in check by severe pruning in late winter.

For such a large plant, A. aconitifolia is surprisingly graceful. The leaves are deeply lobed and elegantly cut. The inconspicuous flowers produce orange berries at the end of summer. A.grandulosa brevipedunculata is less vigorous, and has toothed leaves that are usually three-lobed. In summer on a hot wall the plant will produce blue berries that persist after the leaves have fallen. A. g. b. 'Elegans' is less vigorous and has a white and pink variegation. A. megalophylla has large, dark green leaves, composed of many leaflets, giving it a very different character to the other plants in the genus. It is slower-growing, but will make 10m (35ft). Black berries are borne in autumn. **10–15m (35–50ft).**
✽ ☼ ☁ SC

APIOS AMERICANA

This herbaceous twiner should be more widely used. The small, lightly scented, pea-like flowers have tight, upright heads – each with a muddy pink helmet around a pale browny-purple face. Let it twine around a structure where the flowers can be seen at close quarters. **2m (6½ft).**
✽ ☼ ☁ TW

ARISTOLOCHIA

A genus containing both hardy and tender, evergreen and deciduous, twining climbers. The tender species have the more showy flowers. The flowers are without petals and are shaped like a smoker's pipe with a curled stem. This has earned some species the name 'Dutchman's pipe'. The tender, evergreen A. littoralis is a vigorous plant with heart-shaped leaves and large maroon flowers with white patterning, 10–13cm (4–5in) across. A. macrophylla is hardy, and the light green, large, heart-shaped leaves give it an architectural quality that is ideal for a pergola or a tripod. **5–10m (15–35ft).**
✽ ⌂ ☼ ☁ TW EG

ASARINA

A genus of tender perennials with twining leaf stalks and a soft downy feel.
A. erubescens (syn. Lophospermum erubescens) has pink flowers with a white throat, that are reminiscent of foxglove flowers. Easily grown from seed, it will flower in its first year, so it may also be treated as an annual. It can be grown through a trellis without overpowering either the screen or other plants. It looks good when grown up through shrubs with purple foliage – a copper-beech hedge for example, which, incidentally, will also provide it with protection during the winter. A. scandens (syn. Maurandya scandens) is also easily raised from seed and comes in colours from purple and pink to white. If sown early, it will produce a mass of flowers from midsummer until the first hard frost. Grow it through shrubs, among herbaceous plants, or up a wigwam of canes. **2–3m (6½–10ft).**
⌂ ☼ ☁ TW

BERBERIDOPSIS CORALLINA

This is a weak, twining, evergreen climber. Its pendent clusters of round, red flowers look best against a wall, but it will need to be tied to wires. In the garden it will climb through surrounding shrubs. Flowers are produced from summer to late autumn. The oval leaves are dark green and toothed. It prefers a humus-rich soil, in a sheltered spot out of direct sunlight. **3–4m (10–13ft).**

 TW EG

BOUGAINVILLEA

This is an evergreen, thorny climber. The many hybrids range in colour from warm apricot-orange (*B.* × *buttiana* 'Golden Glow') and brash pinks and scarlets (*B.* × *b.* 'Scarlet Queen') to the cool *B. glabra* 'Snow White' which has fine green veining in the bracts. A vigorous plant when grown in frost-free climates, in frost-prone areas it can be grown in a pot and sheltered over the winter. Prune it hard back after flowering. While dormant, keep it fairly dry and out of freezing conditions. Under cool conditions it loses its leaves. Compost needs to be neutral to slightly acidic. **5–7m (15–25ft).**

 TW

CAIOPHORA ACUMINATA

A curious perennial twiner. The detail inside the orange flowers invites you to tip one up for a closer look, but beware – it is covered in stinging hairs from flower buds to stems. The pointed leaves are finely cut and well spaced along the narrow stems. Grow it through a twiggy support and show it off for its own sake. **2m (6½ft).**

 TW

CAMPSIS

Flamboyant, deciduous, self-clinging climbers that are only successful in frost-free situations. *C. grandiflora* has large, trumpet-shaped flowers of vibrant orange. Cut back vigorous growth in spring. It benefits from lots of sunshine and the warmth of a sunny wall. However, in such a site it will need to be tied in to wires. Poor soil will reduce its vigour and encourage flowering. *C.* × *tagliabuana* 'Madame Galen' has tubular flowers, mellow orange within, and a creamier orange on the outside. **7m (25ft).**

 SC

CANARINA CANARIENSIS

A winter-flowering, herbaceous twiner suitable for frost-free climates or heated conservatories. Veined, reddish-orange, bell-shaped flowers are produced in succession through the winter. In summer it dies down and is dormant, so keep it dry. It may need tying to get it to grow against a wall. **2–3m (6½–10ft).**

 TW

CELASTRUS ORBICULATUS

This vigorous, deciduous twiner needs to be grown on a large wall or tree. In autumn the leaves turn a brilliant butter-yellow. The flowers are insignificant, except for a showy display of red seeds. Buy either a hermaphrodite plant or grow male and female plants close together. **14m (45ft).**

 TW

CLEMATIS

This genus has more than 200 species and 250 cultivars of herbaceous plants and twining climbers. They may be early- or late-flowering. For winter-, spring- and early summer-flowering species and cultivars, prune immediately after flowering. For all later-flowering types, cut

ABOVE: **Campsis *x* tagliabuana 'Madame Galen' produces a blaze of orange trumpets.**

back to 30–40cm (12–16in) in late winter or early spring. All hybrid clematis are at risk from wilt. When wilting is seen, cut back to ground level. Always plant the stem of the clematis 10cm (4in) deep, to help the plant regenerate if later attacked by wilt. Plenty of water in the summer will help keep them healthy.

LARGE-FLOWERED HYBRIDS

The large-flowered clematis hybrids are among the showiest of garden plants. They include *C.* 'Beauty of Worcester': double, lavender-blue flowers; early-flowering with some flowers later on. **2–3m (6½–10ft).** *C.* 'Duchess of Edinburgh': double, white flowers with a green tinge on the outer petals; early-flowering. **2–3m (6½–10ft).**

ABOVE: **Clematis alpina** *has foliage that remains attractive long after the flowers have finished.*

C. 'Gipsy Queen': single, purple flowers; late-flowering. **3m (10ft)**. *C*. 'Hagley Hybrid': single, lilac-pink flowers; late-flowering. **2–5m (6½–16ft)**. *C*. 'Huldine': single, white flowers with a mauve reverse (the flowers face upwards, making these hybrids ideal for growing in low positions); late-flowering. **3–4m (10–13ft)**. *C*. 'Jackmanii' has one of the strongest colours: single, blue-purple flowers; late-flowering. **3m (10ft)**. *C*. 'Nelly Moser': single, rose-mauve flowers bleaching with age (and sepals with a dark central stripe); early-flowering. **3–5m (10–16ft)**. *C*. 'Ville de Lyon': single, crimson flowers produced over a long period; early-flowering. **2–3m (6½–10ft)**.

❄ ☀ ☁ TW

C. ALPINA

A deciduous, spring-flowering species, which needs occasional thinning. The single, blue flowers appear among light green leaves, and silky seedheads provide winter interest. Tolerant of shade, it looks good with evergreen shrubs or hedges. 'Frances Rivis' bears large, pale lavender-blue flowers, whilst those of 'Ruby' are a purple-blue shade. **2–3m (6½–10ft)**.

❄ ✄ ⌂ ☀ ☁ ☁ TW

C. ARMANDII

An evergreen, spring-flowering clematis. The fragrant, white flowers are borne in clusters, and show up well against the dark green foliage. Grow it on a pergola in a sheltered area to get the best of the delicious scent. 'Apple Blossom' has pink-tinged buds. Prune to keep it within bounds. **3–5m (10–16ft)**.

❄ ☀ ☁ TW EG

C. 'BILL MACKENZIE'

This is a vigorous plant, and in late summer thick 'lemon-peel' flowers appear amidst a tangle of grey-green foliage. Be prepared to cut out great bundles of stems in spring. **3–4m (10–13ft)**.

❄ ☀ ☁ TW

C. CIRRHOSA

This early-flowering clematis produces open cup-shaped flowers. These are cream in colour, sometimes flecked with red, and appear singly or in clusters from late winter to early spring, followed by eye-catching seedheads. *C. cirrhosa*'s leaves are tinged with bronze underneath. **2.5–3m (8–10ft)**

❄ ☀ ☁ TW

C. ✕ DURANDII

This plant is a cross between a large-flowered climbing clematis and a small-flowered herbaceous clematis. The rich blue flowers go well with pink and white roses and the yellow *Hemerocallis* 'Marion Vaughn'. **1–2m (3–6½ft)**.

❄ ☀ ☁ ☁ TW

C. FLAMMULA

This plant produces a mass of frothy, white flowers in late summer and autumn, which turn to silky seedheads in the winter. Cut almost to the ground in late winter. The new shoots will find their way up through trellis or large shrubs. **3–5m (10–16ft)**.

❄ ☀ ☁ TW

C. MACROPETALA

The attractive double flowers of this early-flowering, deciduous clematis have sepals that become paler towards the middle of the flower. The foliage is divided and light, and very little pruning is needed. 'Markham's Pink' has dusky, pink flowers; and 'White Moth' is aptly named, both for its colour and the whispy texture of its sepals. **1.5–2m (5–6½ft)**.

❄ ☀ ☁ TW

C. MONTANA

Possibly the most vigorous clematis, in spring it is covered in flowers. Prune after flowering to prevent it becoming a tangled mess. 'Alexander' bears scented, white flowers; 'Picton's Variety' is a mauve-pink and is less vigorous than 'Tetrarose', which has deep, pink blooms. All flower well on a shady wall. **7–12m (25–40ft)**.

❄ ☀ ☁ ☁ TW

C. 'PERLE D'AZUR'

A vigorous, small-flowered plant bearing open, bell-shaped, azure flowers from midsummer to autumn. **3m (10ft)**.

❄ ☀ ☁ TW

C. TEXENSIS GROUP

This group of hybrids are small-flowered and can be left to grow among herbaceous plants. They flower in late summer. *C.* 'Duchess of Albany' has open, upright, soft pink flowers and *C.* 'Gravetye Beauty' has upright, red flowers. Cut down to 40cm (16in) in late winter. **2–3m (6½–10ft)**.

❄ ☀ TW

C. VITICELLA GROUP

A late-flowering group of hybrids. Varied in vigour, they produce some of the best crimsons and dark purples. *C.* 'Abundance' has rose-pink flowers, freely borne. *C.* 'Alba Luxurians' is a vigorous plant with white flowers. It has a long flowering season, and is shown to best advantage when grown through the dark foliage of *Sambucus nigra* 'Guincho Purple'. *C. viticella* 'Purpurea Plena Elegans' is an old hybrid that has fully double flowers of soft purple. It associates well with the mauve flowers of *Hydrangea villosa*. **2–3m (6½–10ft)**.

❄ ☀ ☁ TW

COBAEA SCANDENS (Cup-and-saucer plant)

This tender perennial is more often grown as an annual. It will quickly smother trellis or a pergola with a dense covering of dark foliage. The large, streaky purple, bell-shaped flowers sit in a green calyx, giving the plant its common name. *C.s. alba* has greeny white flowers. Sow seeds indoors in spring and plant out when the risk of frost has passed. **4–6m (13–20ft)**.

⌂ ☀ TW

CODONOPSIS

A genus of herbaceous twiners. *C. clematidea* bears china-blue, bell-shaped flowers,

which show orange and purple markings on the base of the petals. Leaves are small and rounded. It will climb through herbaceous plants or small shrubs in light shade, and dies down in the winter. **1–1.5m (3–5ft)**. *C. convolvulacea* bears more open, blue flowers. It is a delicate-looking plant that thrives in frost-prone climates. **2m (6½ft)**.

❄ ☁ TW

CONVOLVULUS

C. altheoides is a herbaceous plant that is often seen scrambling across the ground, but its twining stems will curl around twiggy supports. The open, pink, bell-shaped flowers complement the silver-grey leaves.

BELOW: **Cobaea scandens alba** *produces sumptuous, bell-shaped flowers.*

It can be invasive, but is easily grown in a pot if this is a problem. It is hardy when established in the ground. **1m (3ft)**.

❄ ☀ TW

DICENTRA TORULOSA

This half-hardy annual, a relative of the bleeding heart (*D. spectabilis*), climbs over bushes or through hedges, covering them in small, blue-tinged leaves. The yellow flowers are followed by knobbly, red seed-pods. The tangled growth is suited to wilder parts of the garden. **2–3m (6½–10ft)**.

✳ ☀ TW

ECCREMOCARPUS SCABER

In frost-free climates this climber is a perennial, but it is easily raised as an annual from the seeds produced in the puffed-up pods. The flowers, held in sprays, are tubular, 2–2.5cm (¾–1in) long, and are usually orange, but red and yellow forms exist. They are borne from midsummer onwards. The leaves are small with deep veins, giving a crinkly appearance. Try growing it through a large shrub or hedge in an informal setting. **2–3m (6½–10ft)**.

❄ ✳ ☀ TW

FALLOPIA BALDSCHUANICA
(Russian vine)

Also known as the mile-a-minute vine, this deciduous twiner is extremely vigorous. From late summer onwards, the frothy mass of tiny, pinkish-white flowers makes an impressive sight. It can look good simply grown up a post or used as a curtain of hanging shoots along a rope tied between posts or trees. Cut back severely each winter **12m (40ft)**.

❄ ☀ ☁ TW

FICUS PUMILA (Creeping fig)

A relative of the rubber plant, this climber attaches itself with short aerial roots. Small, heart-shaped leaves age to elongated ovals. It makes good green cover outdoors in frost-free climates and is controlled by regular cutting back. In frost-prone areas it can be grown in a conservatory and used to support the more colourful *Tweedia caerulea* (syn. *Oxypetalum caeruleum*). **2–8m (6½–25ft).**

 SC EG

HEDERA (Ivy)

Ivies will often grow where nothing else will, as they are tolerant of deep shade and dry, poor soils. Self-clinging evergreens, they will cover the ugliest surfaces in greenery, as short aerial roots 'glue' the plant to a surface. There are hundreds of ivies, each with different leaf shapes and characteristics that make them suitable for a range of uses. **2–10m (6½–35ft).**

H. COLCHICA 'Sulphur Heart'

Large heart-shaped leaves with a lime-yellow centre and a dark green edge. This ivy is good for ground cover, but it will climb up walls. The colours are best in light shade. **5m (16ft).**

✳ ☀ ☁ SC EG

H. HELIX

This common ivy has given rise to many excellent garden cultivars. 'Adam': mottled leaves, veined white and grey-green. It is similar to 'Glacier' and 'Eva', but is more likely to suffer frost damage. **1–2m (3–6½ft).** 'Atropurpurea': leaves turn a dark, coppery colour in cold weather. Grow it where you can see it close up in the winter. **4–5m (13–16ft).** 'Buttercup': butter-yellow leaves when grown in full sun (the colour is lost in shade). This ivy makes a good background to a green foliage border. **2m (6½ft).** 'Duckfoot': leaves shaped like a duck's foot. It may be used for *faux* topiary. **1.5m (5ft).** 'Goldheart': leaves with a distinct, yellow centre. Grow in good light to keep the colour. Cut out green shoots, as they will eventually take over. **5–6m (16–20ft).** 'Green Ripple': leaves have feathery fingers, and outstanding light green veins. **1–1.5m (3–5ft).** 'Ivalace': medium-sized, glossy leaves with a crinkly edge. **1–1.5m (3–5ft).**

✳ ☀ ☁ ☁ SC EG

HUMULUS LUPULUS 'AUREUS' (Golden hop)

A herbaceous climber with hand-sized, yellow-green leaves that look good against a dark background of evergreens. The male form is more common, although hops are only produced on female plants. It looks stunning combined with the lavender-blue *Clematis* 'Elsa Späth'. It will twine through shrubs, trees and trellis, but if grown against a wall it will need to be tied in to vertical wires. Prune to ground level before the new growth appears in spring. **6m (20ft).**

✳ ☁ ☁ TW

HYDRANGEA

H. anomala petiolaris is a tough, deciduous climber. The flat, white flower-heads, borne in early summer, are made up of small, fertile flowers surrounded by larger, sterile ones. Stems cling using aerial roots, and eventually develop into thick trunks. Secure young shoots when establishing it against a wall or fence, or grow it through a tree. **15m (50ft).** Evergreen *H. serratifolia* has less showy flowers. **10m (35ft).**

✳ ☀ ☁ ☁ SC

IPOMOEA

I. lobata is a mid- to late-flowering climber with deeply lobed leaves and racemes of dark red flowers that fade through orange to a creamy white. This is a tender perennial, but it is often grown as a seed-raised annual. A useful container plant, it will twine through early-flowering shrubs or strong perennials. **2–3m (6½–10ft).**

The genus also includes some annual climbing relatives of convolvulus, which have large flowers and heart-shaped leaves. Grow them in a conservatory or a sheltered position outdoors. *I. tricolor* 'Heavenly

BELOW: **Humulus lupulus *'Aureus'* is a useful plant to mix with dull evergreens.**

Blue': sky-blue, trumpet-shaped flowers, with white centres. **2–3m (6½–10ft)**. *I. nil* 'Scarlet Star': cherry-red flowers with a white centre. **2m (6½ft)**.

 ☼ TW

JASMINUM

A fragrant genus (with a few exceptions), available in many colours. Jasmines require conditions that are not too dry.

J. OFFICINALE

A very vigorous, deciduous climber, and one of the most sweetly scented. Pinnate leaves create a tangle of foliage behind full heads of small white flowers. It is tolerant of quite hard pruning. **5–7m (15–25ft)**.

✳ ☼ TW

J. POLYANTHUM

Not quite as vigorous or hardy as *J.officinale*, but deliciously scented and an exceptional conservatory plant. **3–5m (10–16ft)**.

⚬ ☼ TW EG

LABLAB PURPUREUS (Hyacinth bean)

This tender perennial is usually grown as an annual in frost prone areas. It is a fast-growing, twining climber bearing racemes of purple or white flowers in summer, followed by shiny red pods. **6m (20ft)**.

 ☼ TW

LAPAGERIA ROSEA

This classy evergreen has elongated, bell-shaped flowers typically in pink and crimson. The overlapping petals have a waxy texture, the white flowers of *L. r. albiflora* have the appearance of alabaster. A neutral to acid soil is best. The flowers are borne in late

summer and autumn. In frost-free climates, grow it outside in dappled shade through evergreen foliage; or indoors in a shady, moist environment. **5m (16ft)**.

⚬ ⌒ ⌒ TW EG

LATHYRUS (Ornamental pea)

The ornamental peas are tendril climbers. They can be split into two groups: the annuals, which include sweet peas, and the perennials. **1.5–4m (5–13ft)**.

Perennials include the everlasting pea, *L. grandiflorus*, which bears large, lightly-scented, crimson-purple flowers, and *L. latifolius*, which produces a mass of magenta-pink flowers through summer and early autumn. **2m (6½ft)**. *L. l.* 'White Pearl' has larger, white flowers. Lord Anson's pea, *L. nervosus*, bears small, clear blue flowers against rounded, grey-green leaves. It needs protection during very cold weather. **1.5–2m (5–6½ft)**.

The annuals include *L. chloranthus*, with lime-green flowers, and *L. tingitanus*, with purple and crimson flowers. The popular sweet peas are derived from *L. odoratus*. There is a wide variety of cultivars, ranging from white to blue and red, with plants of heights from **40cm (16in)** up to **2m (6½ft)**. Sow outdoors in spring or under gentle heat in late winter. Harden off, and plant out early. Regular dead-heading will ensure a continuing supply of flowers.

✳ ☼ ⌒ TW

LONICERA (Honeysuckle)

This genus of evergreen and deciduous twiners includes many scented plants. Some showy ones, although not scented, are also well worth growing. Fragrant

honeysuckles produce their strongest scent in the evening. If they are cut back in spring most respond with a greater show of flowers. **2–20m (6½–65ft)**.

L. × BROWNII 'Dropmore Scarlet'

This deciduous, or semi-evergreen, unscented honeysuckle produces clusters of tubular, red flowers. **2–3m (6½–10ft)**.

✳ ☼ ⌒ TW

L. JAPONICA

'Aureoreticulata' is grown for its yellow-veined leaves, but it can be knocked back in a hard winter. It is one of the less vigorous honeysuckles. The evergreen 'Halliana' is hardier and more vigorous, bearing scented white flowers, which fade to yellow from mid to late summer. **10m (35ft)**.

✳ ☼ ⌒ TW

L. PERICLYMENUM

This is the common, deciduous honey-suckle, or woodbine. There are several cultivars, in vibrant shades of yellow, orange and pink. The early-flowering Dutch honeysuckle, 'Belgica', has fragrant flowers, purplish-pink outside and yellow within. 'Graham Thomas' has a long flowering season and cream flowers. The late-flowering Dutch honeysuckle, 'Serotina', bears fragrant, purple flowers with a cream interior. **5–6m (15–20ft)**.

✳ ☼ ⌒ TW

L. × TELLMANNIANA AND L. TRAGOPHYLLA

These deciduous honeysuckles bear large, bright yellow flowers. They look impressive when grown through a holly (*Ilex*) or another large evergreen. **5m (16ft)**.

✳ ☼ ⌒ ⌒ TW

MUTISIA

A genus including some evergreen, tendril climbers that bear daisy-like flowers. They require shelter in frost-prone climates. *M. decurrens* is difficult to establish, but showy when growing well. It likes a cool, moist root run. For intense colour, grow it up a wall with the scarlet-flowered *Tropaeolum speciosum*, using ivy as a background and support. **3m (10ft).**

M. oligodon is a more subdued, clear pink. Grow it among shrubs to protect the root-stock from the worst of the frost. *Cotinus coggygria* 'Purpureus' makes a good foil for its pink flowerheads. **1.5m (5ft).**

❋ ☀ ☁ **EG TW**

PARTHENOCISSUS

These vigorous climbers are grown for their foliage. However, they can invade gutters and tiles, and are best cut away from roofs annually. The classy *P. henryana* has dark green leaves with silver-grey markings. It is shade tolerant and produces good autumn colour. The cultivar *P. himalayana* 'Purpurea' contrasts well with the greeny-yellow leaves of *Hedera colchica* 'Sulphur Heart'. *P. quinquefolia* (Virginia creeper) is tougher and equally fast-growing. It has five-fingered leaves, split to the base, which turn crimson and purple in autumn.

P. tricuspidata (Boston ivy), also has brilliant autumn colours. The young leaves are neat and compact; mature ones are large-lobed and shiny. **10–15m (35–50ft).**

❋ ☀ ☁ ☁ **SC**

PASSIFLORA (Passion flower)

A large genus of vigorous, tendril climbers with showy flowers. In hardiness, they

ABOVE: *The arrangement in each passion flower (Passiflora) is exquisitely complex.*

range from *P. caerulea* which stands several degrees of frost to *P. quadrangularis* which needs a winter temperature above 10°C (47°F). Overwintered cuttings of less hardy types can be treated as biennials and planted out in early summer on a trellis or wall, where they will produce their flowers until the colder days of autumn. Grow less hardy types in a conservatory, cutting back laterals in spring. **4–8m (15–25ft).**

The common *P. caerulea* has palmate leaves and intricate flowers with white petals and purple and white filaments. The flowers are short-lived, but are produced continually during the summer. In warm conditions, large, egg-shaped fruits appear in autumn. *P. edulis* is similar, but tender, and produces edible passion fruit. The tender *P. coccinea* has scarlet flowers, which are made more intense by a white centre. **3–4m (10–13ft).**

The *P. quadrangularis* (granadilla), bears complicated flowers with a corona of long, white-, blue- and purple-banded filaments. The large fruit are edible and the leaves are oval in shape. **8m (26ft).**

❋ ⚹ 🏠 ☀ ☁ **TW EG**

PILEOSTEGIA VIBURNOIDES

This is one of a few self-clinging ever-greens. Slow-growing, it is tolerant of shade and its long, leathery leaves show up the frothy, cream flowerheads borne in late summer. **5m (16ft).**

❋ ☀ ☁ ☁ **SC EG**

PLUMBAGO AURICULATA

This evergreen bears bright, sky-blue flowers from midsummer to late autumn – longer under cover. As a conservatory plant, the woody stems can be tied to horizontal wires. In the garden, train it against a wall or let it climb through shrubs. Try it among the silver leaves of *Elaeagnus angustifolia*. Cut it hard back when bringing in for winter protection. **3m (10ft).**

🏠 ☀ ☁ **TW EG**

RHODOCHITON ATROSANGUINEUS

Although strictly a tender perennial, it is easily grown as an annual from seed. Often called the parachute plant, due to its flower shape, it climbs by twisting its leaf stalks around its support. The purple tubular flower hangs below a red calyx.

Plant it among shrubs with variegated foliage such as *Fuchsia magellanica molinae* 'Sharpitor', which has white variegation. **2–3m (6½–10ft)**.

   TW

ROSA (Rose)

The number of climbing and rambling roses is too great to cover in full, so the list below constitutes a personal choice of varying sizes, colours and fragrances. It is divided into three sections: climbing species roses; hybrid climbing roses; and rambling roses. All climb by means of thorny, arching stems, and most require some form of training. Species roses are wild roses that have not been hybridized; some are the parents of hybrid ramblers and climbers. Most roses need spraying to prevent disease, and a feed with a rose fertilizer in spring will also improve the quality of the plants. In wilder parts of the garden, a degree of neglect can be tolerated, athough the result may be the production of fewer flowers.

CLIMBING SPECIES ROSES

R. brunonii, (the Himalayan musk rose), is exceptionally vigorous: grey-green foliage and large clusters of scented, white flowers, 2.5–5cm (1–2in) across. In cold areas there is a risk of frost damage. **10m (33ft)**. *R. filipes* 'Kiftsgate' is also very vigorous: large, scented cream flowers. If wrongly situated, it will be difficult to control, but if sited by a large tree or on a bank, it can be left to romp away. **10–15m (33–50ft)**. The late-flowering musk rose, *R. moschata* – not strictly a wild rose – is less vigorous: sprays of single, white flowers with a strong fragrance from late summer to mid-autumn. It is ideal for a pergola. **3–4m (10–13ft)**. *R. mulliganii* (*R. longicuspis*) is another large rose: dense heads of small, white flowers appear in early summer. The attractive foliage is glossy and deeply toothed and will persist during mild winters. **8–10m (25–35ft)**. *R. wichuraiana* is the parent of many rambling roses: small, scented white flowers in midsummer. **5–6m (15–20ft)**.

  TW

HYBRID CLIMBING ROSES

These tend to have larger flowers and a longer flowering period than both the climbing species and the ramblers – producing new blooms after the first flush. Shorten last year's sideshoots annually and occasionally remove old thick stems completely. Otherwise, prune as necessary to maintain a shapely plant. Prune between midwinter and early spring, but do not be afraid to prune in summer to maintain a good shape. *R.* 'Blush Noisette': repeat-flowering from late summer to mid-autumn; clusters of small, double, cupped, pink flowers with a rich clove scent. Grow in the warmest part of your garden. **4m (13ft)**. *R.* 'Danse du Feu': mid- to late-flowering; rounded, double, scarlet flowers. Plant at the back of a border of orange crocosmias and hot-coloured daylilies (*Hemerocallis*) for a fiery effect. This rose will tolerate shade. **3m (10ft)**. *R.* 'Golden Showers': mid- to late-flowering; large, double yellow flowers that fade with age. Another good rose for shade. Grow up a post or large tripod. **3m (10ft)**. *R.* 'Madame Grégoire Staechelin': mid-flowering; masses of large, scented, double pink flowers. **5–6m (15–20ft)**. *R.* 'Maigold': early-flowering, then intermittently through the season; bronze-yellow flowers go well with the purple-blues of early clematis such as *Clematis* 'Elsa Späth'. Foliage is strong, glossy and disease-resistant. **3–4m (10–13ft)**. *R.* 'Mermaid': large, open, single flowers with a boss of rich amber stamens. It benefits from a sheltered position and needs little pruning. Foliage is disease-resistant. **5–6m (16–20ft)**. *R.* 'Parkdirektor Riggers': semi-double, crimson flowers throughout the season. The foliage is dark and glossy. For a rich effect, grow with *Clematis* 'Jackmanii'. **4m (13ft)**.

  TW

RAMBLING ROSES

These have a more graceful habit than climbers. Prune occasionally to remove old stems at the base and encourage flowering shoots. The flowers are usually small and are produced only once in the season. They are ideal for arches, bowers and pergolas, where they create a fragrant ambience. *R. banksiae* 'Lutea' has a charm that sets it apart: early-flowering; hanging sprays of tiny, yellow flowers. Foliage is light green, small and open. It is an ideal partner for *Wisteria sinensis* or purple *W. × formosa* 'Black Dragon'. **9–10m (30–35ft)**. *R.* 'Bobbie James': mid-flowering; massive heads of fragrant, cream flowers. It needs a big pergola or tree, or grow it horizontally along a post-and-rail fence. **8–10m (25–35ft)**. *R.* 'Crimson Shower': double flowers of strong crimson. Try *Solanum jasminoides* 'Album' or the pink-budded *Jasminum officinale* as climbing partners. **4m (13ft)**. *R.* 'Paul's Himalayan Musk': late-flowering; trailing shoots bear sprays of lightly scented, blush-pink double rosettes. This is another good pergola plant. **9–10m (30–35ft)**. *R.* 'Phyllis Bide': an unusual repeat-flowering rambler; small, yellow flowers with a slight orange-pink flush. **3m (10ft)**. *R.* 'Rambling Rector': mid-flowering; small, semi-double, cream flowers with a very enjoyable fragrance. **5–6m (15–20ft)**. *R.* 'Wedding Day': huge clusters of flowers that are yellow in bud, but quickly turn white when they open. It is one of the most fragrant ramblers. **9–10m (30–35ft)**.

❋ ☀ ☁ TW

SCHISANDRA RUBRIFLORA

This is the showiest of the climbers in this genus. The deciduous leaves are oval, and in early summer it produces pendulous red flowers, even on a shady wall. The flowers are followed by strings of red fruit. Both male and female plants are needed

BELOW: *Its fresh white flowers give* **Solanum jasminoides** *'Album' a sparkling elegance.*

for a good set of berries. Shoots can be trained along horizontal wires or left to twine up vertical wires where upright growth is desired. **5–6m (15–20ft)**.

❋ ☀ ☁ ☁ TW

SCHIZOPHRAGMA INTEGRIFOLIUM

A deciduous, self-clinging relative of the hydrangea with conspicuous, white bracts surrounding the large, flat flowerheads, to 30cm (1ft) across. The oval leaves are dark green and finely toothed. To establish against a wall, use lead-headed nails to hold the branches firmly in place. **10m (33ft)**.

❋ ☁ ☁ SC

SENECIO CONFUSUS

This tender evergreen has twining stems and wavy-edged, arrow-shaped leaves. Purple-tinged when young, it bears daisy-like, orange flowers, in sprays of five or six, 4cm (1½in) across. Grow it outside in frost-free climates, otherwise keep it as a conservatory plant. Cuttings (easily rooted in late summer) may be grown on during winter, then planted out in summer, to enhance the effect of a border of tender perennials. **3m (10ft)**.

🏠 ☀ ☁ TW EG

SOLANUM

S. jasminoides is a semi-evergreen, blue-flowered relative of the potato. 'Album' bears white flower clusters through summer into autumn. Neither are hardy in frost-prone climates and benefit from a wall's protection. Overwintered 'Album' cuttings may be planted among shrubs, or grown through a tall, evergreen hedge. **6m (20ft)**.

S. crispum 'Glasnevin' is also frost-prone, but usually shoots again from low

down. The flowers are a blue-purple with a yellow 'eye'. Evergreen in sheltered locations, it will need to be tied in to wires when grown up a wall. **5–6m (15–20ft)**.

🗡 🏠 ☀ TW EG

SOLLYA HETEROPHYLLA
(Australian bluebell)

A twining climber that produces clusters of pale-blue flowers from spring to autumn, and, if temperatures do not fall too low, through winter as well. In areas prone to severe frosts, it is a good conservatory or cold-greenhouse plant. Train its stems through a trellis screen or a twiggy shrub. **1.5–2m (4½–6½ft)**.

🏠 ☀ ☁ TW

THUNBERGIA ALATA (Black-eyed Susan)

A cheery, twining plant bearing orange-yellow flowers with a distinct, dark brown centre. This is a perennial that is usually grown as an annual. It needs a warm, sheltered site. Let the air and soil warm up before planting out young seedlings. The shoots will need canes or wire to climb up; otherwise plant them against a wall that gets plenty of sun at the foot of a climber such as honeysuckle. This hides the bare stems of the honeysuckle and gives support to the thunbergia. **2–3m (6½–10ft)**.

🏠 ☀ TW

TRACHELOSPERMUM JASMINOIDES

There are very few fragrant evergreens, and this twining perennial is one of the best. The white flowers are fragrant. Growing it over an arch will make the most of the scent. Where there are severe frosts, it needs the protection of a wall. **9m (30ft)**.

❋ ☀ ☁ ☁ EG TW

TROPAEOLUM

A flamboyant genus that includes the annual climbing nasturtium, *T. majus*. The perennial *T. speciosum* has dramatic scarlet flowers followed by blue berries. The leaves are lobed and their stems curl around twigs, helping to support the plant. It is suited to shady walls, but creeping rhizomes can become a nuisance once it is established. Plant in leafy, humus-rich soil and keep the roots cool. Grown through ivy or a yew hedge, it makes a showy display. **3m (10ft)**.

    T. tuberosum is another perennial with showy flowers, but softer in style and colour. The spurred flower changes from red at the spur to a warm yellow at the mouth. The flowers are poised at the end of dark, narrow, arching stalks which hold them away from the leaves, which appear to be a scaled-down version of nasturtium foliage. Although recommended for sunny locations, it can thrive on a shady wall. It flowers from midsummer to the first frost. The potato-like tubers should be buried 25cm (10in) deep and mulched well in frost-prone areas, or lifted and stored in frost-free conditions. **2.5m (8ft)**

✳ ⚐ ☀ ☁ ☁ TW

T. MAJUS (Nasturtium)

Many dwarf and compact cultivars are now available, but the original large-flowered climbers take some beating. Easily raised from seed annually, they will scramble through shrubs, cover unsightly wasteland, and make good container plants. The plant is also edible: seeds are pickled as capers, and leaves and flowers can be added to salads. Check for caterpillars and their eggs, and pinch out blackfly-infested shoots. They can be sprayed with an insecticide, but

avoid this if you intend to eat the nasturtiums. **3m (10ft)**.

✳ ☀ TW

TWEEDIA CAERULEA
(OXYPETALUM CAERULEUM)

A herbaceous, twining climber with greyish leaves and tubular, five-petalled, pale-blue flowers, fading to purple. Long, swollen seedpods develop after the flowers. Grow under glass in frost-prone areas. **1.5m (5ft)**.

⚐ 🏠 ☀ TW

VITIS (Grape vine)

A genus that includes some bold foliage plants as well as the common grape vine, *V. vinifera*. All climb by tendrils and are tolerant of quite severe pruning in winter. The bleeding that results from late pruning is not harmful.

    V. 'Brant' provides a rich autumn leaf colour that looks good as a background. The leaf veins remain green, showing up the bronze-red of the leaves. **7m (25ft)**.

    Large-leaved *V. coignetiae* will reach the top of a large tree; when pruned it makes a good plant for a pillar or pergola. The leaves turn red and orange in autumn, each leaf turning at a different time to make a glowing patchwork of colours. **15m (50ft)**.

    V. vinifera 'Purpurea' has burgundy leaves that are a good foil for whites, such as *Clematis flammula*, and soft yellows, such as *Helianthus* 'Moonlight'. Full sun gives the best colour. **7m (25ft)**.

✳ ☀ ☁ TW

WISTERIA

This vigorous twining climber produces hanging racemes of fragrant, pea-like flowers which can be shown off through

careful pruning. Each leaf is made up of 14 or so leaflets, making for dense foliage when out of flower. Left unchecked, it will become a tangle of wiry stems, so establish a framework of main branches from the start; this makes subsequent pruning easier. Train evenly spaced shoots up a wall, using vertical wires, or canes, which will break away when crushed by the thickening stems. Cut the ends off the leading shoots when they reach the limits of your area. Cut the next year's sideshoots back to three buds in late summer, to encourage flower-bud production and to create short, outward-facing spurs. In late winter, cut out any long regrowth. Regular pruning allows wisteria to be grown in a confined space. It can also be grown as a free-standing shrub. Initially grow it up a cane, then form the sideshoots into a frame of horizontal branches. Prune as for wall-trained plants.

    Though the flowers are fairly openly spaced, *W. floribunda* produces one of the longest racemes, 70–100cm (3½–4½ft). It climbs in a clockwise direction. Numerous Japanese cultivars range from pink to violet and lilac-blue: 'Alba' bears white flowers that look good against a dark, evergreen background; 'Multijuga' has lilac flowers.

    W. × *formosa* 'Black Dragon' has purple flowers which look impressive when grown through the white 'Alba'. *W. frutescens* has shorter racemes of lilac-purple flowers. Produced on the current season's growth, they are borne for a longer period than *W. floribunda*. *W. sinensis* twines in the opposite direction to *W. floribunda*, and produces a sparse second crop of flowers in late summer. 'Prolific' has long racemes of lilac flowers, freely produced. **9m (30ft)**.

✳ ☀ TW

Index

Page numbers in *italics* indicate illustrations.

ACKNOWLEDGMENTS

Author's acknowledgments
Special thanks to those who offered locations for the projects and who were so generous with their time and hospitality. They were Michael Rand, Julia Parker, Marianne Majerus, Mr and Mrs Malone, Toff and Georgina Milway (extra thanks Georgie, the cakes were delicious), The Pottery, Conderton, Gloucestershire; Mr and Mrs Paice at Bourton House Gardens, Bourton on the Hill, Moreton in Marsh, Gloucestershire. GL56 9AE; also thanks to Sherston Parva Nursery, Malmesbury Road, Sherston, Wiltshire, SN16 0LL, tel: 01666 840623 for the clematis. A big thanks to Barbara, my very patient wife, for the typing of the text.

Publisher's acknowledgments
The publisher would like to thank the following photographers and agencies for their kind permission to reproduce the photographs in this book:

1 Mayer/Le Scanff/The Garden Picture Library; 2–3 S & O Mathews; 5 John Glover/The Garden Picture Library; 6–7 Richard Felber; 8 S & O Mathews (The Little Cottage, Hampshire); 9 J C Mayer – G Le Scanff (Jardins de Villandry (37), France); 10–11 Clive Nichols (Pyrford Court, Surrey); 11 Jerry Harpur (Mr & Mrs John Casson, London); 12 left Marianne Majerus; 12 right Graham Strong; 13 J C Mayer – G Le Scanff (Le Baquè (47), France); 14 Marianne Majerus (Chenies Manor, Buckinghamshire); 15 Sunniva Harte (Mr & Mrs Orchard, Corner Cottage, Sussex); 16 John Glover; 16–17 S & O Mathews (Barnsley House, Gloucestershire); 18 & 19 Brigitte Perdereau; 20 Andrew Lawson; 21 Sunniva Harte (RHS Wisley, Surrey); 22 Richard Felber; 23 left John Glover; 23 right Jerry Harpur; 24–25 Dominique Vorillon; 27 Georges Leveque; 28 Marianne Majerus (Woodpeckers, Warwickshire); 29 S & O Mathews (Little Court, Hampshire); 30 left Marianne Majerus (Red Gables, Hereford & Worcestershire); 30 right Jerry Harpur (Designer: Tessa Hobbs, Suffolk); 31 Jerry Harpur (Eastgrove Cottage Garden, Worcestershire); 32 Roger Foley (Colonial Williamsburg, USA); 33 Sunniva Harte (Mr & Mrs Orchard, Corner Cottage, Sussex); 34 Christian Sarramon; 34–35 Brigitte Perdereau; 36–37 Jerry Harpur (Designer: Diana Ross, London); 37 Marianne Majerus (Designers: Charles Jencks & Maggie Keswick); 42 S & O Mathews

(Cleveland House, Sussex); 43 Marianne Majerus; 44–45 Earl Carter; 46 Marianne Majerus (Little Cottage, Hampshire); 47 Marianne Majerus (Clinton Lodge, Sussex); 48–49 John Glover (Queen Eleanor's Garden, Winchester); 50 left Dency Kane (Dean Riddle Garden, Lanesville, NY, USA); 50–51 Dency Kane (Marla Gagnum Garden, East Hampton, NY, USA); 56 J C Mayer – G Le Scanff (Festival International des Jardins de Chaumont-sur-Loire (41), France. Landscape Gardener: Monika Gora); 57 Georges Leveque (Barnsley House, Gloucestershire); 58 left Clive Nichols (Designer: Olivia Clarke); 58 right J C Mayer – G Le Scanff (Festival International des Jardins de Chaumont-sur-Loire (41), France); 59 Andrew Lawson (Gothic House, Oxfordshire); 60 Richard Felber; 60–61 Andrew Lawson; 61 Roger Foley (Designer: Margaret Atwell); 62 Marianne Majerus; 63 Andrew Lawson (Hadspen House, Somerset); 64 Andrew Lawson; 65 Jerry Harpur (Designer: Bob Clark, California, USA); 72 Jerry Harpur (House of Pitmuies, Tayside, Scotland); 73 Marcus Harpur (Mjr.& Mrs John Allfrey, Castle Hedingham, Essex); 74 & 75 Brigitte Perdereau; 76 left Jerry Harpur (Moorlands, Crowborough, Sussex); 76 right Anne Hyde (Ross Priory, Gartocharn, Strathclyde, Scotland); 77 left Graham Strong; 77 right Brigitte Thomas/The Garden Picture Library; 78 S & O Mathews (Little Court, Hampshire); 79 Clive Nichols (Barnsley House, Gloucestershire); 82 Richard Felber; 83 Richard Felber; 85 Georges Leveque; 86 Clive Nichols (Barnsley House, Gloucestershire); 87 Neil Campbell-Sharp; 88 Dency Kane (New York Botanical Garden, USA); 90 Andrew Lawson; 92 Patrick McLeavey.

The following photographs were taken specially for Conran Octopus by Marianne Majerus: pages 25, 26, 38–39, 40–41, 52–53, 54–55, 64–65, 66–67, 68–69, 70–71, 80–81.

We apologize in advance for any unintentional omission and would be pleased to insert the appropriate acknowledgment in any subsequent edition.